Cambridge Elements

Elements in Political Philosophy
edited by
Cécile Laborde
University of Oxford
Steven Wall
University of Arizona

CIVIL AND UNCIVIL DISOBEDIENCE

Candice Delmas
Northeastern University

CAMBRIDGE
UNIVERSITY PRESS

Shaftesbury Road, Cambridge CB2 8EA, United Kingdom

One Liberty Plaza, 20th Floor, New York, NY 10006, USA

477 Williamstown Road, Port Melbourne, VIC 3207, Australia

314–321, 3rd Floor, Plot 3, Splendor Forum, Jasola District Centre,
New Delhi – 110025, India

103 Penang Road, #05–06/07, Visioncrest Commercial, Singapore 238467

Cambridge University Press is part of Cambridge University Press & Assessment,
a department of the University of Cambridge.

We share the University's mission to contribute to society through the pursuit of
education, learning and research at the highest international levels of excellence.

www.cambridge.org
Information on this title: www.cambridge.org/9781009659147

DOI: 10.1017/9781009659130

© Candice Delmas 2026

When citing this work, please include a reference to the DOI 10.1017/9781009659130

First published 2026

A catalogue record for this publication is available from the British Library

ISBN 978-1-009-65914-7 Hardback
ISBN 978-1-009-65915-4 Paperback
ISSN 2976-5706 (online)
ISSN 2976-5692 (print)

Civil and Uncivil Disobedience

Elements in Political Philosophy

DOI: 10.1017/9781009659130
First published online: April 2026

Candice Delmas
Northeastern University

Author for correspondence: Candice Delmas, c.delmas@northeastern.edu

Abstract: What is wrong with disobedience? What makes an act of disobedience civil or uncivil? Under what conditions can an act of civil or uncivil disobedience be justified? Can a liberal democratic regime tolerate (un)civil disobedience? This Element presents the main answers that philosophers and activist-thinkers have offered to these questions. It is organized in three parts: Part I presents the main philosophical accounts of civil disobedience that liberal political philosophers and democratic theorists have developed and then conceptualizes uncivil disobedience. Part II examines the origins of disobedience in the praxis of activist-thinkers: Henry David Thoreau on civil resistance, anarchists on direct action, and Mohandas Gandhi and Martin Luther King Jr. on nonviolence. Part III takes up the question of violence in defensive action, the requirement that disobedients accept legal sanctions, and the question of whether uncivil disobedience is counterproductive and undermines civic bonds.

Keywords: civil disobedience, uncivil disobedience, protest, resistance, direct action

ISBNs: 9781009659147 (HB), 9781009659154 (PB), 9781009659130 (OC)
ISSNs: 2976-5706 (online), 2976-5692 (print)

Contents

Introduction

Civil disobedience is a crucial tool in the activist's toolbox. From the Freedom Rides, which sought to desegregate interstate transportation in the Jim Crow South, to mass die-ins and roadblocks for climate justice, campaigns of civil disobedience can catalyze change. But civil disobedience also raises profound questions. For activists and organizers, these questions are strategic in nature: Is civil disobedience likely to advance the cause, and, if so, at what cost? For social scientists, the central questions are empirical: Does civil disobedience work – how and why? Philosophers, finally, have tended to approach civil disobedience from a different perspective, one centered on its permissibility: Under what conditions is civil disobedience an ethically sound pursuit?

At the heart of civil disobedience is a violation of law, which, on many philosophical accounts, poses a threat to the social and legal order and therefore requires justification. Especially in liberal democratic regimes, where people have a say in political matters and possess the right to dissent, engaging in civil disobedience seems fraught. How can it be acceptable to contest the democratic will through lawbreaking, especially when one could express one's discontent peacefully and lawfully? Disobedience under democratic conditions appears inherently uncivil – a disruptive and reckless way of dissenting. In response, philosophers defending disobedient activism have argued that it is precisely the civility of civil disobedience that transforms a violation of law into a potentially permissible act. The disciplined, self-restrained character of civil disobedience expresses the activist's respect for democracy and for law and thus disarms concerns about the destabilizing potential of disobedience.

Neither criminal nor revolutionary, civil disobedience is ordinarily defined as a conscientious, nonviolent act contrary to the law, undertaken in public by agents who do not evade legal sanctions and who aim to persuade the majority to bring about a change in law or policy. Unlike criminal agents, civil disobedients engage in a selfless and essentially political act. Unlike revolutionaries, they accept the legitimacy of the politico-legal system in which they are acting; they seek reform within the confines of the system, not subversion of that system.

But what about uncivil disobedience? How do we distinguish between civil and uncivil acts? Are there ever circumstances in which uncivil disobedience is morally permissible? What is the value (if any) of uncivil, as opposed to civil, disobedience? Can liberal democratic regimes tolerate (un)civil disobedience?

This Element addresses these questions and more. It is organized in three parts. Part I, "Theorizing Disobedience," presents the main philosophical accounts of civil disobedience that liberal political philosophers (Section 1) and democratic theorists (Section 2) have developed, before conceptualizing uncivil disobedience (Section 3). Part II, "Practicing Disobedience," examines the origins of disobedience in the praxis of activist-thinkers: Henry David Thoreau on civil resistance (Section 4), anarchists on direct action (Section 5), and Mohandas Gandhi and Martin Luther King Jr. on nonviolence (Section 6). Part III, "Justifying Uncivil Disobedience," takes up the question of violence in defensive action (Section 7), the requirement that disobedients accept legal sanctions (Section 8), and the question of whether uncivil disobedience is counterproductive and undermines civic bonds (Section 9).

• • •

Before proceeding, some terminological clarifications are in order. One of the key terms in any discussion of disobedience is *resistance*. Resistance is a broad concept; I use it to designate a range of dissident activities by individuals or collectives who are motivated by and express opposition to the dominant system of values, norms, rules, laws, and practices. Resisters perceive features of the dominant system as unjust and oppressive and aim to: correct or impede injustice, disrupt oppressive power relationships, promote justice or some other ideal of the good life, and/or enact a different world. Resistance thus covers much more than disobedience, civil or uncivil. It also includes consciousness-raising, organizing, fundraising, canvassing, leafletting, picketing, and other activities that – whether legal or criminalized – seek to build social movements. Resistance may also involve bearing witness, speaking up, and calling out, activities that may foster movements but above all seek to establish the truth. Finally, resistance may be militant and revolutionary, aimed to oust an occupier, overthrow a dominant system (such as apartheid), topple a government, or eliminate the state, through more or less violent means.

Given the focus on unlawful acts of resistance, it is useful to distinguish these from other unlawful acts. I use the label of *principled disobedience* to designate lawbreaking that is conscientious – that is, deliberate and motivated by principles of political morality. Principled disobedience is thus distinct both from criminal disobedience and from acts of "deviance" that are subversive yet not necessarily conceived by the deviant as resistance.[1] That being said, the principled character of disobedience doesn't necessitate "pure" motives. Principled disobedience is compatible with mixed goals; a principled disobedient acts on the basis of conscience but may simultaneously be engaged in thrill-seeking, revenge, or the pursuit of self-interest. The digital disobedience of hacktivist groups like Anonymous appears mixed in this

---

[1] See, e.g., Bourdieu, 1977; Foucault, 1983; and Hartman, 2019.

way: one of their distributed-denial-of-service attacks against PayPal and Visa was called Operation: Avenge Assange, laying bare the group's desire for payback, even as it attempted to vindicate the conscience-driven disobedience of the activist journalist Julian Assange.

I have already mentioned another key term: *civil disobedience*. Civil disobedience should be understood as an "essentially contested concept," which different thinkers have theorized in different ways.[2] Sections 1 and 2 lay out the two central approaches, beginning with the liberal philosophical account, because it undergirds the public understanding of civil disobedience in Western societies. On this conception, which is premised on the recognition of state legitimacy and the attendant duty to obey the law, civil disobedience is a conscientious, public, and nonviolent breach of law undertaken to correct injustice and carried out by actors willing to accept legal consequences. Republican and radical democratic theorists view matters differently. Because they understand civil disobedience as an expression of collective self-determination designed to democratize society, they tend to relax the criteria of civility.

Uncivil disobedience may be conceptualized as the negative of civil disobedience – that is, as an act of principled disobedience that fails to satisfy the criteria of civility outlined by liberal philosophers and commonly assumed by the public. Covertness, anonymity, property destruction, the use of force in self-defense, evasion of sanctions, and offensiveness (where civil disobedience is expected to be, if not polite, then at least dignified and respectful) are thus common marks of incivility. A disobedient act is generally uncivil if it checks one of these boxes, and especially more than one. The concept of uncivil disobedience thus covers various disparate types of unlawful resistance that have in common only their violation of the requirements of civility. Examples include political riots, guerrilla street art, unauthorized whistleblowing, hunger strikes, and a range of environmental disobedience, such as pipeline sabotage, occupation of polluting construction sites, and deflating the tires of gas-guzzling automobiles.

Protest is a narrower category than resistance. While resistance may not be primarily communicative, protest is always a speech-act, designed to address a public. Marches, demonstrations, and flash mobs are protests. Civil disobedience, as a public act, always encapsulates a communicative protest. For their part, some, but not all, acts of uncivil disobedience may be interpreted as protests. Defacing a statue commemorating an enslaver is aptly deemed protest. In contrast, neither breaking into a laboratory to rescue animals nor performing an abortion where it is illegal is a protest. These are not designed as speech-acts; they are deeds – acts of rescue or of care.

---

[2] Scheuerman, 2021.

That which the agent disobeys and opposes may be a *norm*, a *rule*, or a *law*. During the AIDS epidemic, gay people who publicly displayed their affection in kiss-ins disobeyed heteronormative social norms that stigmatize and pathologize gay love. Students who skipped classes to attend Fridays for the Future events disobeyed school rules against truancy in order to demand action against climate change. People who refused to comply with public health measures to contain the spread of COVID-19 disobeyed the law. Although it is perfectly appropriate to speak of each as a case of disobedience, my focus in this Element is on the third category, lawbreaking. It is this last kind of disobedience to which philosophers have devoted much attention, seeing it as a more serious and more high-stakes violation than its rule- and norm-targeted counterparts. Of course, laws often formally codify institutional rules and social norms, so that skipping school and publicly displaying queer love may be legally sanctioned by truancy laws and laws against "indecent behavior." In many situations, then, disobedience contravenes norms, rules, and laws all at once.

In some cases, disobedience targets specific *individuals* rather than laws or institutions. For instance, protesters threw milkshakes at far-right politicians (a tactic dubbed "milkshaking") in the United Kingdom during the 2019 European Parliament election. In 2022, after the draft majority opinion that denied a constitutionally protected right to abortion was leaked to the public, hundreds of demonstrators protested outside the homes of the conservative Supreme Court Justices who authored and supported the draft opinion.

Finally, disobedience may be *direct* or *indirect*. Civil rights activists who sat in at whites-only lunch counters directly disobeyed the laws they protested – laws mandating racial segregation in public facilities. Direct disobedience is necessary for constitutional test cases, that is litigation that challenges the constitutional validity of the law disobeyed. In contrast members of the activist group Extinction Rebellion engage in indirect disobedience when they block roads. These activists aren't opposed to traffic regulations; rather, they transgress against these in order to protest state inaction with respect to climate change and state support of highly polluting industries.

With these terms in place, let's dig into some theories of disobedience.

Part I Theorizing Disobedience

1 Civilizing Disobedience

From the late 1950s through the early 1970s, the United States was shaken by antinuclear, antiwar, and civil rights protests. Amid the Vietnam War, draft resistance was common, and the peace movement gained considerable strength. The Civil Rights Movement built enough momentum to drive the passage of civil rights legislation in 1964 and 1968 and voting rights legislation in 1965. But this was also an era when Black Americans loudly protested police brutality and poverty, leading to outbreaks of civil unrest and riots, More than 700 such incidents were recorded between 1964 and 1971, peaking after Martin Luther King Jr.'s assassination by a white supremacist in 1968. The 1970s also saw a good deal of political violence – though less than in Western Europe – with an estimated 2,500 bombings between 1971 and 1972 by left-wing groups such as the Weather Underground and Black Liberation Army. Faced with such deep unrest, authorities and a sizable portion of the public condemned *all* protests by appealing to law and order.

It is in this context that a clutch of Anglo-American philosophers, trained in the analytic tradition and sharing basic liberal commitments, began theorizing civil disobedience. A cast including Hugo Adam Bedau, Ronald Dworkin, Carl Cohen, Michael Walzer, and John Rawls broadly sympathized with the antinuclear, antiwar, and civil rights causes and even approved of some disobedient acts deployed in their service.[3] But these authors also worried about the destabilizing potential of the protests they were witnessing and strongly condemned riots and left-wing political violence.

1.1 The Problem of Disobedience

The liberal inquiry into civil disobedience begins with lawbreaking.[4] Disobedience is found to pose a problem because violations of law destabilize society and shake confidence in the rule of law. As Socrates put it when refusing his friend Crito's offer to help him escape jail and evade his death sentence, deliberately contravening the laws of Athens would amount to "intending the destruction" of the polity.[5] For any individual violation of law signals the permissibility of mass lawbreaking, which itself threatens the state's ability to maintain the peace and justice.

---

[3] Bedau, 1961, 1991; Cohen, 1971; Dworkin, 1978, 1985; Walzer, 1982; Rawls, 1999. See Forrester (2019) for the background.

[4] The rest of this section and the next one draw from Delmas and Brownlee (2024, § 1.2–1.3 and 3).

[5] Plato (2002, 50a-b).

Another way to describe these concerns is to say that disobedience is presumptively wrong because it violates the moral duty to obey the law, which philosophers refer to as *political obligation*. The law, on this view, holds sway not only because the state possesses the coercive power to enforce it. Subjects are bound by *duty* to submit to the law, when the state that issues it is a legitimate one.[6] Meanwhile, subjects have a right not only to disobey but to overthrow illegitimate government. Disobedience is thus a problem only in legitimate states.

The exact nature and contours of legitimacy are contested, of course, but democracy, insofar as it recognizes subjects' fundamental moral equality and enables self-government, is usually seen as a condition and marker of political legitimacy. Disobedience is an especially acute concern in democracies because it expresses an individual's willingness to place their judgment above that of the sovereign majority. This is so even in the face of unjust law. For the point of political obligation is at least in part to explain why subjects have a moral duty to obey the law even when disobedience appears morally right given the law's injustice.

So, if, as Rawls puts it, there is "no difficulty in explaining why we are to comply with just laws enacted under a just constitution," and if political obligation binds us to follow even unjust laws provided they are issued by a legitimate state, can disobedience ever be permitted on the liberal view?[7] Rawls wondered as much, writing, "The real question is under which circumstances and to what extent we are bound to comply with unjust arrangements."[8] Rawls suggests that injustice may reach "certain limits" beyond which the subject is no longer bound to obey, even in an otherwise reasonably just state. With political obligation weakened or dissolved, there is room for unlawful forms of dissent, including civil disobedience.

1.2 Liberal Civility

Given the "problem" of disobedience, liberal theorists have sought to show that not all disobedience destabilizes society, undermines the rule of law, and flouts democracy. Their solution is *civility*. By disobeying civilly, one demonstrates one's goal of addressing the community and one's adherence to the system's legitimacy and overall respect for law. Civil disobedience can thus be understood to stand "within the limits" or "at the boundary of fidelity to law," as Rawls puts it.[9]

Rawls defines civil disobedience as a "public, nonviolent, conscientious yet political act contrary to law [that is] usually done with the aim of bringing about a change in the law or policies of the government" by addressing the sense

---

[6] While the dominant view is that legitimate political authority entails political obligation, some philosophers like Edmundson (1998) and Applbaum (2019) argue that legitimacy is a necessary but not sufficient condition for political obligation.

[7] Rawls (1999, p. 308).   [8] Rawls (1999, p. 308).   [9] Rawls (1999, p. 322).

of justice of the majority and undertaken by an agent who accepts the legal sanctions.[10] Civil disobedience meets four criteria, three of which Rawls states directly: it is carried out publicly, nonviolent, and undertaken by an agent who willingly accepts the legal sanctions for her lawbreaking. In my view, the normative constraints of civility further imply that the agent acts with decorum.

The disobedient act's requirement of *publicity* stems from the communicative purpose of civil disobedience: It must aim to send a message to the broader society. With this in mind, the act must be witnessable. It must be done in the open, which usually means a public space – a town square, say, rather than an official's driveway. Many also argue that the agent must not conceal her face or identity. Some theorists even hold that civil disobedients must give authorities advance notice of their planned action and, when appropriate, seek a permit to protest. Finally, many theorists hold that the disobedient act must be public in the more specialized sense that the appeal it makes must be based on widely accepted principles of political morality.

The requirement of *nonviolence* prohibits the use or threat of physical force against persons, which, for Rawls, would muddy the disobedient act's legibility as a public address. Most liberal theorists, as well as many disobedients, further argue that nonviolence prohibits coercion – the forcing of actions – as well as damage to property. Again, this reflects civil disobedience's goal of pleading with and persuading the public. (Section 7 explores challenges to this orthodox view.)

Agents' willing acceptance of the legal consequences of their lawbreaking – *non-evasion*, as I call it, though I mean something broader, as I'll explain in Section 8 – is another mark of civility and a defining criterion of civil disobedience. Whereas the duty to accept punishment focuses on the moment of the trial, "non-evasion" refers to a series of demands on civil disobedients even before judicial proceedings are underway: agents must not dodge or resist law enforcement; they must comply with criminal and court proceedings and accept their outcomes. Non-evasion is crucial to the goal of demonstrating the agent's respect for the rule of law and endorsement of the overall legitimacy of the system in which she is acting. (Section 8 motivates the conceptual shift from the narrower duty to accept punishment to the broader requirement of non-evasion and defends departures therefrom.)

I believe a fourth mark of civility is at play in the standard liberal conception, albeit implicitly: *decorum*, which holds that civil disobedients ought to behave in a dignified manner, by following the conventional social scripts that spell out the ways of showing respect in their society. This mark explains why some

---

[10] Rawls (1999, p. 320).

public, nonviolent, and non-evasive acts of disobedience are nonetheless denied the label "civil," on the grounds that they are seen as, say, offensive, obscene, or blasphemous – in violation of decorum. (Section 8 explores this requirement's intersection with non-evasion in the form of courtroom decorum, and Section 9 defends the intrinsic value of fitting expressions of distrust and anger.)

Civility thus understood appears in stark contrast to criminality and revolution. People who commit criminal offenses typically break the law for self-interested reasons, potentially violently, and almost always covertly, with intent to evade legal sanctions. And while revolutionary actors are, like civil disobedients, moved by moral and political principles to break the law, revolutionaries tend to share with criminals the willingness to use violence and the desire to evade of punishment. Criminal offenders and revolutionaries, then, act outside the "limits of fidelity to law."

In contrast, by satisfying the weighty demands of civility, the agent can demonstrate her respect for law and assuage the public's fear of disorder and resentment at the disruption that disobedience creates. Some acts of civil disobedience may even earn praise.

1.3 Justification and Role of Civil Disobedience

Rawls offers both an account of conditions under which acts of civil disobedience can be justified and a general account of the role of the practice in a liberal democratic society. In his view, acts of civil disobedience can be justified only if they are undertaken: (1) to target serious and long-standing injustice, (2) as a last resort, and (3) in coordination with other groups with similar grievances.[11] I'll explain all three in turn.

First, Rawls, along with Dworkin and Jürgen Habermas, restricts the target of civil disobedience to serious and long-standing or entrenched injustices – paradigmatically, violations of basic rights. In Rawls's view, the chance that civil disobedience will succeed rests on the clarity of the injustice protested: the overwhelming majority must be able to recognize the violation as an injustice, given widely accepted and valid principles of political morality. For instance, racial segregation, which in the United States imposed second-class-citizen status on African Americans, constitutes an incontrovertible and entrenched injustice in a way that socioeconomic inequality does not. Both segregation and socioeconomic inequality undermine the fair value of political liberties, but only one is a blatant violation of basic rights that anyone in agreement with democratic principles would be enjoined to recognize. Similarly, Dworkin and

---

[11] Rawls (1999, pp. 326–329).

Habermas argue that civil disobedience should focus on constitutional rights, not matters of policy such as nuclear or climate regulations.[12]

Critics, including some liberal philosophers, have sought to expand the justificatory conditions beyond this narrow frame, to include protests against economic inequality such as Occupy Wall Street in the United States and the Indignados movement in Spain. Other critics contend that novel – which is to say, not widely accepted – principles of justice and non-political principles of morality can ground permissible civil disobedience, for instance on behalf of animal welfare. Indeed, the actions of the animal rights movement, as well as other major emancipatory movements like Black Lives Matter and #MeToo, reveal that civil disobedients often seek to transform common-sense political morality rather than issue calls for change on its basis.

The second justificatory requirement – that civil disobedience be undertaken as a last resort – has become an article of faith. In a liberal democratic society where the right to vote and the right to dissent are recognized and protected, people should not turn to disobedience lightly. Essentially, civil disobedience is thought to be permissible to the extent that majorities overlook people with legitimate grievances. Where lawful channels are less than wholly effective in addressing the majority – a condition that is especially likely to prevail among minorities – civil disobedience may be acceptable.[13] How do we know that agents are overlooked? Rawls suggests that if past actions, including by other persons similarly situated, have shown the majority to be immovable or apathetic, then further attempts may reasonably be thought unnecessary, and the dissenter may undertake civil disobedience.

Some critics defend a moral right to civil disobedience that does not require exhausting all legal means first, as we'll see in Section 8 (§2). Other critics argue that civil disobedience itself may be overlooked by an immovable majority, and that in such cases, uncivil disobedience may be considered a last resort after civil disobedience has been exhausted.

The third justificatory requirement demands that those minority social groups equally justified in resorting to civil disobedience against injustice coordinate their civil disobedient actions with each other. This condition is designed to regulate the overall level of dissent and minimize disruption. It is also supposed to heighten the act's chances of success by avoiding a cacophony of small civil disobedient protests that would tax the public's attention, ensuring instead maximum participation in well-planned actions.

Critics have argued that while coalition-seeking is generally good strategy for activists, it makes little sense to condition the justification of civil disobedience

---

[12] Dworkin, 1985; Habermas, 1985.   [13] Rawls (1999, pp. 327–328).

on it. Groups may not have the time to coordinate with other groups, or they may have security concerns that prevent them from inviting affinity groups to participate. Furthermore, a protest must not necessarily be large in order to attract attention. For instance, Prescription Addiction Intervention Now (PAIN), an advocacy group founded by artist Nan Goldin in response to the opioid crisis and specifically targeting the Sackler family for their responsibility, staged a die-in at the Metropolitan Museum of Art in 2018, scattering in the rotunda fake prescription bottles and mock one-dollar bills labeled "Oxy." Performance protests like this one led large museums to remove the Sackler name from their galleries and endowments. Such highly choreographed actions require only small numbers of participants.

•••

Liberal philosophers recognize that justified civil disobedience does not necessarily undermine the rule of law and can instead strengthen the social and legal order. As Rawls has it, civil disobedience serves "to inhibit departures from justice and to correct them when they occur," thereby enhancing justice.[14] Civil disobedience offers a special protection from majoritarian encroachments on individual rights, functioning as a defense or redress mechanism – a corrective device to fix rights violations.

Liberal philosophers assume in their reflections on civil disobedience the validity of the constitutional principles that regulate society, and which activists must appeal to. They conceive of civil disobedients as gadflies, intervening in the public sphere to remind the society of its professed commitments to worthy principles of political morality. Dworkin thus analogized civil disobedients to constitutional court justices engaging in constitutional disputes but from below. On this view, when the law's validity is doubtful, civil disobedience is constitutionally acceptable – even welcome – and may, in fact, not involve lawbreaking at all, given the law's possible unconstitutionality.[15]

Habermas similarly conceives of civil disobedients as breaking the law to protest "against the transgression of valid constitutional principles."[16] He presumes a constitutional liberal democratic society regulated by acceptable principles of justice. At the same time, he understands civil disobedience as a valuable and "necessary component of [the constitutional liberal democratic society's] political culture," because of its contribution to public deliberation. In fact, Habermas's recognition of civil disobedience as "the guardian of legitimacy" is also at the root of democratic accounts of civil disobedience.[17] Let's turn to these.

---

[14] Rawls (1999, p. 336).   [15] Dworkin (1985, pp. 104–116).   [16] Habermas (1985, p. 107).
[17] Habermas (1985, p. 103).

2 Democratizing Disobedience

Picture the 1963 March on Washington; the 1989 Tiananmen Square protests; and the occupations of Manhattan's Zuccotti Park in 2011, Istanbul's Gezi Park in 2013, and Athens's Syntagma Square in 2017. These were mass protests brought about by social movements tapping into collective anger and democratic yearning. In the twenty-first century, chants of "This is what democracy looks like!" reflect the protestors' conviction that civil disobedience and democracy are deeply intertwined.

Where liberal theorists tend to read civil disobedience through an individualistic, moral, and constitutional lens, democratic theorists frame civil disobedience first and foremost as collective political action. While the lawbreaking element of civil disobedience – including the breach of unjust law undertaken as constitutional challenge – recedes in importance, its democratic power comes to the fore. Democratic theorists reject liberals' view of civil disobedience as a check on majoritarian government's perceived threat to basic rights and argue instead that civil disobedience is itself a form of democratic empowerment.

Within democratic theory, there are three principal approaches to civil disobedience: republican, deliberative, and radical. This section addresses each in turn.

2.1 Republicanism: Civil Disobedience as Democratic Renewal

Hannah Arendt, a contemporary of the US-based liberal theorists discussed in Section 1, interpreted the disobedient antiwar and civil rights activism of her day as an essentially democratic mode of political action. In so doing, she turned the liberal approach on its head. Whereas liberal theorists sought to show that the civility of civil disobedience could defuse its destabilizing potential, Arendt argued that what really disrupts social order is not civil disobedience but instead the state's exclusion of certain groups from the political process, which makes rebellion inevitable.[18] Mass disobedience, in Arendt's view, always occurs under unstable political circumstances but ultimately steadies society by reenacting the social contract and thus strengthening civic bonds. Civil disobedience, then, is both a symptom of and the remedy to an unstable legal order.

Arendt emphasizes the political, rather than moral or legal, aspect of disobedience by tying it to the spirit and practice of voluntary association. Here, voluntary association is the germ cell of democratic political power because it fosters collective deliberation and active civic engagement. Arendt does not define civil disobedience, and she does not distinguish it from revolution. She

---

[18] Arendt, 1972.

instead views both as modalities and even exemplars of democratic action, efforts to found a new shared public space where political freedom can appear, that is, where human beings can live and act together and start something new. As historical case studies, she looks to the American Revolution, the Paris Commune of 1871, and the Hungarian revolt of 1956. Like these, the Civil Rights and antiwar movements were opening the space to usher in new beginnings.

2.2 Deliberative Democracy and Civil Disobedience

Deliberative democracy, a school of thought influenced by Rawls and Habermas, emphasizes the role of reason and communication in public life in general and democratic decision-making in particular. Rawls argues that discussion should be informed by mutually acceptable reason-giving, while Habermas highlights inclusive dialogue premised on mutual respect. While Rawls's own account of civil disobedience is not of the deliberative school, Habermas articulates a hybrid liberal-deliberative account. Like Rawls, he conceives of civil disobedience as a guardian of constitutional principles. However, he also stresses civil disobedience's essential contribution to democratic deliberation and will-formation, with disobedients promoting more radical interpretations of the system of rights. Such a contribution is valuable on the deliberate view because civil disobedients do not aim to undermine the constitutional principles that underpin political legitimacy but rather to deepen and extend them.

This might sound like the liberal account, which also legitimizes civil disobedience to the extent that it supports the constitutional order. But there is a crucial difference. Where liberal accounts deem legitimate disobedience which guards rights from the infringements of democratic majorities, deliberative theorists argue that disobedience can be legitimate even in the absence of clear rights violations to the extent that it stimulates public deliberation concerning foundational principles of free societies. For instance, civil disobedience can inspire a public conversation about material and political inequality and failures of recognition and reciprocity, issues that redound to the value of our political rights, even when they are not technically violated.[19] What is more, deliberative democrats welcome debates, reassessments, and revisions of fundamental rights through public action aimed at achieving a novel political consensus.

The deliberative approach, then, focuses on the citizen as an agent within the democratic process. William Smith, who has articulated the most complete and

---

[19] Young, 2001; Fung, 2005.

compelling deliberative treatment of civil disobedience, looks beyond constitutional rights and instead to the rudiments of citizenship when he speaks of the "capacity" of civil disobedience "to enhance epistemic processes through which publics weigh up competing claims and perspective."[20]

This epistemic purpose is especially crucial in the face of "deliberative breakdowns or process-related failings in the public sphere," as Smith writes.[21] The actions of Occupy Wall Street exemplify this sort of epistemic work. The US constitutional order does not attempt to prevent economic inequality and therefore does not recognize such inequality as unjust. Yet political power is concentrated in the hands of the wealthiest, resulting in the alienation of most people from their power within the framework of self-government. This was the message of the Occupiers, who sought to appeal to the constitutional principle of political equality, even in the absence of rights violations. Similarly, the US Dreamers – undocumented-immigrant youth who have been granted legal status without a path to citizenship – have protested their exclusion from participation in the public sphere as antidemocratic, given the impact that the state's decisions have on them. For a last example, La Via Campesina, an anti-globalization farmers organization, seeks to put the concerns of landless workers, indigenous people, rural migrants, and certain other populations on the agendas of states, where these concerns are otherwise ignored as a result of "deliberative inertia."[22] In each of these cases, the point of civil disobedience is not to guard justice but to enhance democratic deliberation by triggering processes of epistemic reflection across the public sphere.

2.3 A Radical Theory of Disobedience

Whereas deliberative democrats conceive of democracy as a space of respectful dialogue geared toward the achievement of consensus, theorists of radical democracy conceive of democracy as first and foremost a space of contestation. Further, civil disobedience is central to this struggle. For radical democrats like Robin Celikates, civil disobedience is neither a check on democratic politics nor a remedy for deliberative breakdowns. It is instead, as in Arendt's republican account, democratic agency itself – an assertion and creation of the citizen's power that opens spaces of political possibility. But radical theorists, unlike republicans, further draw on critical theory in their analysis of power and resistance, as they situate themselves within political practice and align their theoretical objectives with the broader goal of emancipation that underpins the movements they study.

---

[20] Smith (2021, p. 106).   [21] Smith (2021, pp. 111–114).   [22] Smith (2013, chap. 2).

According to Celikates, civil disobedience constitutes a form of democratic empowerment, which works by putting forth a "dynamizing counterweight to the rigidifying tendencies of state institutions."[23] That is, civil disobedience confronts the vertical constituted power of state authorities with the horizontal constituting power of the people. Civil disobedience aims at a more inclusive and extensive form of democratic self-rule: it democratizes democracy, from below. On this view grassroots actions are the heartbeat of democracy. Thus, in her study of the Gezi protests of 2013, Çiğdem Çıdam pays close attention to the on-the-ground efforts of political actors to build political friendship and enact democratic action.[24]

Radical theorists' critique of liberal and deliberative accounts is extensive. Radical democrats reject the liberal framing of the problem of civil disobedience, which deliberative democrats share: radical democrats do not assume state legitimacy or political obligation, and they do not conceptualize the constraints of civility as a solution to disobedience's presumptive impermissibility. They also reject the argument that disobedience is justified only on the basis of its appeal to valid constitutional principles. On the radical view, civil disobedience needs no distinctive moral justification. In any case, constitutional principles are unlikely to provide any such justification, as these principles often buttress a violent order rather than safeguard minority rights.

Radical democrats overhaul the liberal conception of civil disobedience first by rebuffing any effort to fix it in amber. Instead, civil disobedience is understood as a constantly evolving concept "not just in theory but also in practice."[25] Celikates thus denounces practically every defining feature of the standard liberal account. Against the publicity requirement (which includes advanced notification to authorities), for instance, he notes that covertness is often essential to the preparation and conduct of civil disobedient action and that anonymity not only protects activists but also can have a powerful symbolic value, as when protesters all don Guy Fawkes masks. He also understands nonviolence as compatible with property damage and civil disobedience as incompatible "not with violence per se, but with an unreflective embrace of violent means that neglects how violence – in addition to potentially harming others – affects and transforms both the subjects and the aims as well as the context of political action."[26] Thus acts of civil disobedience, for radical democrats but not for liberal philosophers, may be covert and destructive.

What radical democrats maintain as the core element of civil disobedience is its communicative function. This function is conceived in collective and

---

[23] Celikates (2014, p. 223).   [24] Çıdam (2021, ch. 6).   [25] Celikates (2021, p. 132).
[26] Celikates (2021, p. 137).

political terms, not through the lens of individual freedom of expression. Hence Celikates defines civil disobedience much more broadly than liberals and deliberative democrats do, as

> an intentionally unlawful and principled collective act of protest (in contrast to legal protest, "ordinary" criminal offenses or "unmotivated" rioting), with which citizens – in the broad sense that goes beyond those recognized as citizens by a particular state – pursue the political aim of changing norms, practices, institutions, and self-understandings (in contrast to conscientious objection, which is protected in some states as a fundamental right and does not seek such change) in ways that should be seen as civil (as opposed to military).[27]

This capacious definition makes plenty of space for activists' experimentation with the practice of disobedience, outside the liberal strictures of civility.

Radical democrats also propose rethinking the notion of civility itself, arguing that liberal civility does covert ideological work to "discredit and discipline" activists.[28] Specifically, radical democrats charge that liberal theory sets up activists to fail by erecting excessively demanding standards for the practice of disobedience. Radical theorists propose instead that civility is not a normative standard of behavior but rather refers to the condition of political membership. A civil act need not be a decorous one; instead, it is an act of *citizenship*, even when the actor is not legally designated a citizen but is, say, a refugee, guest worker, or undocumented migrant. As citizens, disobedients "acknowledge some kind of civil bond with their adversaries, which goes hand in hand with certain forms of self-limitation and self-restraint that exclude military or quasi-military action aiming at the destruction of an enemy."[29] Civility, on this view, is synonymous with political contestation, which involves struggling for recognition and vying for power, rather than the elimination of the opposition.

Finally, radical democrats insist that theorists must take sides in the political struggles of their times. In this respect, they are heirs to the Frankfurt School of critical theory, members of which argued that the philosopher's role is to contribute somehow to the emancipatory struggle that she seeks to theorize. Emmanuel Renault contrasts critical theorists' self-positioning as allies with those who oppose injustice against liberal understandings in which the philosopher is an "impartial" observer.[30] As Karl Marx argued, radical philosophies of resistance should be developed from the bottom up, on the basis of activists' experiences, claims, and practices, so that they can constitute an "organ" of

---

[27] Celikates (2021, p. 134).   [28] Celikates (2021, p. 135).   [29] Celikates (2021, pp. 134–135).
[30] Renault (2015, p. 5).

emancipatory movements.[31] Celikates likewise urges theorists to "learn from the streets," so as to do justice to social movements and facilitate their struggles.

Radical theory thus departs significantly from the more liberal orientation of deliberative theory, but it is important that we not lose sight of areas of agreement. Republican, deliberative, and radical democrats all view civil disobedience as an essential tool for contesting state failures and as a quintessential form of democratic empowerment. Democratic theorists converge on their conception of civil disobedience as a creative, not defensive, mechanism and an expression of popular power.

3 Conceptualizing Uncivil Disobedience

Let us set the stage with a few vignettes.

The radical environmental group Earth First! conducted the first known tree spiking in the Siskiyou Mountains of Oregon in 1983, driving metal stakes into trees on land designated for timber sale by the Bureau of Land Management. Spiking aims to deter logging by making trees nonviable as timber: stakes don't kill the tree, but they damage saw blades and can cause injury to loggers and sawmill workers, so a spiked tree is hazardous to cut down. The activists gave notice of the spiking and marked some of the trees with yellow ribbons to make them easy to find and to minimize the risk of injury to loggers.

During the AIDS epidemic of the 1990s, activists from ACT UP (the AIDS Coalition to Unleash Power) stormed the offices of pharmaceutical companies, spattering walls with fake blood. They also stormed pharmaceutical congresses, heckled speakers and sometimes handcuffed them to force them to listen, and scattered on buffets the ashes of friends who had died of AIDS.

In 1999, 300 unionized famers of the Confédération paysanne led by José Bové and Syndicat des producteurs de lait de brebis (the ewe's milk producer association) gathered at the construction site of a McDonald's restaurant in Millau, a town in the Aveyron department of France. Some of them dismantled the building in construction while others handed out tartines of roquefort. They were protesting the World Trade Organization (WTO)'s decision to authorize US sanctions over the European Union's refusal to import meat from cows raised on growth hormones.

In 2013, Edward Snowden, a contractor working for the US National Security Agency (NSA), stole 1.7 million classified documents. He leaked 200,000 of them to journalists, revealing details of the NSA's massive domestic and international surveillance program.

---

[31] Marx (1963, p. 143).

In October 2022, climate justice activists from Just Stop Oil threw tomato soup over Van Gogh's *Sunflowers* (which was protected by glass) at London's National Gallery before gluing their hands to the wall beneath the painting. A year later, in the same museum, two other Just Stop Oil activists smashed the protective glass panel covering Diego Velázquez's *Rokeby Venus*.

These acts have in common the deployment of illegal tactics for principled ends, including securing environmental sustainability and climate justice, equal access to healthcare, and privacy. Many actors involved were criminally charged and prosecuted. Some were called terrorists. All of these acts have been described, by those who approve of them, as instances of civil disobedience, highlighting their agents' principled, conscientious motivations and situating the disobedients within a venerable historical tradition associated with the likes of Mohandas Gandhi, Martin Luther King Jr., and Rosa Parks.[32]

However, none of these disobedient actions fit the standard liberal account of civil disobedience. Tree-spiking is a potentially dangerous form of sabotage, undertaken clandestinely and anonymously; ACT UP used uncivil and coercive tactics, such as handcuffing and damaging property; the farmers destroyed the McDonald's restaurant in construction (inflicting more than $260,000 worth of damages in today's dollars); Snowden covertly stole and leaked classified information and evaded legal sanctions by fleeing the United States; and while Just Stop Oil activists did not inflict irreversible damage on invaluable paintings, they inflicted economic costs on museums, which were forced to clean up galleries, repair frames and other materials protecting the works, and increase security.

Two roads are open, then, for theorists who are sympathetic to some or all of these actions: insist on the acts' civility or grant their incivility and instead focus on their justifiability. This section presents these two approaches and defends the latter, before briefly showing how arguments in favor of civil disobedience can be extended to justify some acts of uncivil disobedience. (Section 9 further sketches a defense of uncivil disobedience.)

3.1 Insist on Civility or Justify Incivility?

To argue for the civility of actions like those just described involves relaxing the criteria of civility. Some liberal theorists do this, insisting for instance that Snowden was engaged in civil disobedience because he took responsibility for his actions, which appealed to valid constitutional principles for justification and sought to strengthen the rule of law. He avoided punishment but never denied or hid his efforts.[33] For their part, radical democrats need not bend over

---

[32] This section draws from Delmas (2020a).   [33] Scheuerman, 2014; Brownlee, 2016.

backward to accommodate these cases: their capacious vision of civil disobedience can find space for them.

The benefits of incorporating acts of resistance in the category of civil disobedience are clear: to do so not only begins but nearly completes the work of normative legitimation. To say – and be able to persuade others – that the agents above were all engaged in civil disobedience, like Gandhi, Parks, and King, is to deny their lawlessness and to justify their actions at once. So, why do anything else? The fact is that, in the public imagination, civil disobedience is a conscientious, public, nonviolent, non-evasive, and respectful breach of law. Hence many attempts to encompass acts that fail to satisfy the constraints of civility within the category of civil disobedience often fail, at least in the public's eye, for they are perceived to be stretching the common understanding beyond recognition. These attempts' failures by no means suggest they shouldn't be undertaken; to the contrary, I find theorists' efforts to contest and broaden the public conception of civil disobedience very important, as the latter is of course not fixed for eternity. But it is dominant for now.

This is why the second option must be pursued, too. It strikes me as the more fruitful in the short and medium term, because while the common understanding of civil disobedience remains, this second route enables theorists to defend certain acts of principled disobedience on widely accepted grounds. It is therefore a pragmatic move. It counsels setting aside debates about the meaning and constraints of civility, accepting the standard definition of civil disobedience and common presumption that the society is a basically liberal democratic one, and focusing instead on justifying uncivil tactics.

As sketched in the introduction, uncivil disobedience can be conceptualized as the negative image of the standard understanding of civil disobedience. If an act of principled disobedience is civil when it is (i) public, (ii) nonviolent, (iii) non-evasive, and (iv) dignified and respectful, then an act of principled disobedience may be uncivil in virtue of being (i) covert or anonymous, (ii) violent, injurious to persons, harmful to oneself, destructive of property, or coercive, (iii) evasive of law enforcement and legal sanctions, or (iv) offensive, disrespectful, or undignified. A principled disobedient act's failure to meet any one of the criteria of civility is usually sufficient to mark it as uncivil.

José Medina adds nuance to this way of distinguishing between civil and uncivil protests, stressing that the key differences between civil and uncivil acts are "not absolute and categorical, but gradual and contextual."[34] The distinction is "contextual" because civility and incivility can be properly interpreted and assessed only in context – that is, only in light of the social, cultural, and

---

[34] Medina (2020, p. 124, his emphasis).

epistemic norms that govern how people perceive the act in question. The distinction is also "gradual" insofar as civil and uncivil protests should be thought "as being in a continuum, as situated in a wide and heterogeneous spectrum of cases deploying different kinds of confrontation that may challenge legality and norms of civility to a lesser or fuller extent."[35]

The sociocultural variations in perceptions of civility are real. In fact, one of the vignettes above *is* considered paradigmatic of civil disobedience (or "désobéissance civique"), despite the significant property damage involved, to wit: the unionized farmers' dismantling ("démontage") of the McDonald's restaurant, which unfolded undisturbed by the police and then led to a highly mediatic trial.[36] While a number of French people – and the authorities – viewed the action as vandalism ("saccage"), the French public as a whole does not see property destruction as necessarily incompatible with civility, the way the United States does. There is no doubt that a similar action in the United States would have been brutally repressed and branded as "violent extremism" and "domestic terrorism," given the legislation that makes damage to critical infrastructure punishable as terrorism today. The French tradition of resistance, replete with revolutionary and socialist uprisings and the underground resistance to the Nazis, does not involve nor celebrate nonviolence. While anti-imperialist activists in the United States, India, and South Africa looked to Gandhi, King, and Mandela as their models in the twentieth century, their French counterparts turned instead to revolutionaries like Leo Trotsky, Ho Chi Minh, and Che Guevara: nonviolent civil disobedience for the former, armed class struggle for the latter. French activists today tend to view both civil disobedience and sabotage as among a healthily diversified repertoire of tactics rather than as a disjunctive and existential choice. To put it simply, conceptualizing uncivil disobedience is less pressing or useful in societies where the public understanding of civil disobedience and of the permissibility of resistance is already broader and more permissive.

Medina is right: civility and incivility exist on a spectrum. Conformity with certain criteria is objectively ascertainable: whether an act was carried clandestinely, for instance, may be hard to argue. But, in many cases, whether a protest is civil or uncivil will depend on the agent's perceived identity, social position, and goals. Consider how Black American football players' silent protests in solidarity with Black Lives Matter were condemned as disrespectful, unpatriotic, and even traitorous, while silent protests by police officers under the banner of Blue Lives Matter were read as dignified and respectful.

---

[35] Medina (2020, p. 123).   [36] Bové and Luneau, 2004.

If Medina suggests that the distinction between civil and uncivil disobedience is not rigid or fixed, other theorists argue that such distinction is misguided and should be abandoned. For William Scheuerman, defenders of uncivil disobedience "tend to group a vast array of distinctive types of lawbreaking under one amorphous categorical rubric, impeding the suitably complex, nuanced analysis we need."[37] In his view, the very concept of uncivil disobedience functions as a "residual category (meaning, in effect, 'non-CD [civil disobedience],' with CD narrowly and controversially defined)."[38] He continues:

> Placing morally offensive but nonviolent protest, sabotage, armed resistance, vigilantism and whistleblowing under the same conceptual rubric, whatever its other analytic advantages, invites a failure "to distinguish different situations in which different forms of illegal protest and resistance are acceptable."[39]

Such hodgepodge of a concept hinders rather than promotes nuanced analysis of protests and resistant practices and their context-dependent permissibility. What is more, according to Erin Pineda, conceptualizing uncivil disobedience hinders the vital work of reclaiming civil disobedience's subversive power from the claws of the sanitized liberal account which is too narrow and too demanding and distorts the real historical practices of civil disobedience.[40]

One might be tempted to respond to the idea that the concept of uncivil disobedience is an amorphous hodgepodge, that the opposite strategy of broadening civil disobedience also bloats the concept to incorporate "variegated types"[41] that one may deem uncivil, such as politically motivated vandalism and leaks. But proponents of such inclusive approach argue that all these types of conscientious lawbreaking are united by their civil orientation. For Scheuerman, it is an embrace of a shared political project and fidelity to law that makes an act of disobedience civil; for Kimberley Brownlee, it is the act's communicative nature and the agent's willingness to bear the risks of honoring her conscientious convictions; for Robin Celikates, it is the protester's enactment of radical citizenship.[42]

Now what, if anything, unites uncivil disobedience? It is true that the concept groups together diverse types of principled disobedience that all have in common not to fit a narrow concept of civil disobedience, though they might be situated on different points of the spectrum of incivility. But as I noted, operating with the public understanding of civil disobedience is the point of this

---

[37] Scheuerman (2019, p. 982).   [38] Scheuerman (2019, p. 989).
[39] Scheuerman (2019, p. 989). Scheuerman is citing Jubb (2019, p. 956).   [40] Pineda, 2021b.
[41] Scheuerman (2019, p. 989).
[42] Brownlee (2012, chap. 1); Celikates 2014 and 2021; Scheuerman 2015 and 2019.

approach: it challenges the existing normative parameters that make civil disobedience the only acceptable mode of protest and puts new concepts in circulation that point beyond it. Having categorized an act under the umbrella of uncivil disobedience does not tell us very much about it beyond its principledness and perceived and/or deliberate failure to satisfy one or other of the marks of civility. Whereas defenders of civil disobedience have articulated full-throated accounts of the value and role of civil disobedience in liberal democratic societies and defended citizens' moral right to civilly disobey (discussed in Section 8.2), there can be no blanket defense of uncivil disobedience, nor a general moral right to engage in it. But there is no reason to infer from this asymmetry the ineptness of the present account of uncivil disobedience. Far from "impeding the suitably complex, nuanced analysis we need," as Scheuerman criticizes, the underspecification of the concept of uncivil disobedience invites and even requires close-up examination.

Because the concept of uncivil disobedience groups together "variegated types"[43] of principled disobedience, it must be disaggregated. Indeed, a defense of, say, the clandestine provision of abortion services where it is illegal will not tell us much about the circumstances under which property damage inflicted during political rioting might be permissible. Normatively evaluating uncivil disobedience (a fortiori specific acts within distinct situations) requires (a) articulating a political ethics of a given type of uncivil disobedience (such as government whistleblowing, environmental sabotage, political rioting, or hunger strike), with defining features and justificatory conditions; and (b) assessing the specific context in which a particular act takes place, to properly draw the contours of the injustice being resisted (or to confront agents' perceptions with the reality) and to enable us to judge whether the uncivil tactics were well calibrated to the context and end pursued. Close-up judgments will reveal that even among justified acts of a given type of uncivil disobedience, some might, while others will not be undertaken by agents who display fidelity to law and share a commitment to a common political project. In contrast, many theories of civil disobedience make the latter by definition a signal of these things, without being open to the possibility that the disobedience in question be both justified and not designed to signal them.

Finally, from the conceptualization of uncivil disobedience as a negative of civil disobedience, it doesn't follow that the account leaves intact a too-narrow, too-demanding, and sanitized concept of the latter. Rather, characterizing certain acts of principled disobedience as uncivil creates opportunities to expose and denounce the ideological agenda underlying ubiquitous calls for

---

[43] Scheuerman (2019, p. 989).

civility in the liberal mode. As critics of liberal civility note, the powerful often use the injunction to be civil as a way of controlling and silencing activists, casting them in a negative light and prejudicing the public against them – even when their protests are, in fact, peaceful. Calls for civility conceal what Bernard Harcourt calls the "incivility of politics" – the harms it regularly inflicts – and obscure power differentials.[44] Embracing incivility can then be a way to render these dynamics visible by showing that the public sphere is infected by testimonial injustice: only those in power have ready access to a public sphere governed by norms of civility; only they can speak and be heard. Entrenched minorities, meanwhile, lack such access, forcing them to engage in uncivil disobedience. Incivility, then, becomes an index of disempowerment, its recognition a means of foregrounding testimonies that otherwise find no audience.

More directly, incivility can help reveal how the template of civil disobedience is used as a muzzle. Perhaps this is why, despite its negative connotations, the label of incivility has more often been embraced in recent years. Consider the example of the democracy movement in Hong Kong, which took an explicitly and unapologetically *uncivil* turn after the 2014 Occupy Central protest failed to sway the Chinese government. Whereas Occupy Central was modeled on liberal civility, the 2019–2020 Water Revolution saw hundreds of protesters turning out in hard hats to smash the windows of the territory's Legislative Council Complex. One protester scrawled on a wall of the complex, "It was you who taught me that peaceful marches are useless."[45]

Finally, a caveat: albeit useful, the distinction between civil and uncivil disobedience does not fit all acts of unlawful resistance. Indigenous resistance to settler colonialism in North America is a case in point: although typically interpreted as civil or uncivil disobedience, it is often neither. That binary categorization, as Yann Allard-Tremblay argues, presupposes a "shared civic world" – a common public and constitutional order – and frames resistant conduct as concerned with it.[46] But Indigenous activists neither accept nor see themselves as participants in the settler-colonial civic order. Instead, their resistance is grounded in and revitalizes Indigenous sovereignty – that is, ancestral ways of relating to one another, animals, and the land. Thus, the Indigenous activists who resisted the construction of the Dakota Access Pipeline at Standing Rock rejected the labels of "protestors" and "civil disobedients," insisting they were instead "protectors" of water and land.

---

[44] Harcourt, 2012.   [45] Delmas, 2020b.   [46] Allard-Tremblay (2026, p. 90).

3.2 Justifying Uncivil Disobedience

If it is at least sometimes valuable to understand principled disobedience as uncivil, then we should ask whether such disobedience can be justified. This section briefly outlines the possibility of extending arguments in favor of civil disobedience to justify some types of uncivil disobedience. Section 9 will go further by responding to charges that uncivil disobedience is counterproductive and undermines civic bonds and by outlining its unique, positive contributions to supposedly liberal democratic societies.

Recall that, in response to the concern that disobedience violates the moral duty to obey the law, many theorists have pointed out that injustice, when it exceeds certain limits, dissolves political obligation and opens up a space for principled, civil disobedience. Why not uncivil disobedience as well? In previous work, I have urged an expansion of the concept of political obligation to include duties to resist injustice, including by way of civil and uncivil disobedience. My argument is that the same normative principles commonly used to ground the moral duty to obey the law support obligations to resist injustice and sometimes counsel uncivil disobedience.[47]

Recall, too, the liberal argument that civil disobedience can strengthen the recognition, protection, and enforcement of basic constitutional rights. Now consider as well that a disobedient act need not be civil in order to have such effects. For example, Snowden's whistleblowing bolstered the rule of law by exposing serious wrongdoing and abuses by state agents and by promoting governmental accountability. Similarly, the FBI's unconstitutional Counterintelligence Program, better known as COINTELPRO, was ended after the *Washington Post* ran a front-page story about it on the basis of illegal leaks: anonymous members of an activist group, the Citizens' Commission to Investigate the FBI, broke into a bureau office, stole more than a thousand classified documents, and turned them over to reporters. Indeed, in these cases, uncivil disobedience not only promoted justice, it also buttressed the rule of law even as it involved covert lawbreaking. And yet the activists who exposed COINTELPRO were radical peace activists who neither trusted the government nor saw themselves as acting within the limits of fidelity to law. At the very least, such incidents complicate the liberal argument that civility is necessary in order that disobedience not destabilize the social order and the rule of law.

---

[47] Delmas (2018a, chap. 3–6) discusses the natural duty of justice, the principle of fairness, the Samaritan duty, and political membership. Very briefly, these principles require that citizens work to redress unjust institutions, cease benefiting from harmful and exploitative social schemes of cooperation, rescue people from peril, and uphold political associations that respect the dignity of all.

If uncivil disobedience can be a means of promoting justice, it can also be an exercise of democratic politics, following democratic accounts. Disobedience need not be civil in order to highlight democratic deficits, demand inclusion, and combat the rigidifying tendencies of state institutions. Suffragists' uncivil protests in demand of the franchise are a case in point. Although female suffragists' tend to be remembered as civil disobedients (likely due to class privilege), they used tactics that were clearly uncivil. They smashed the windows of London's shopping district, vandalized the Royal Botanic Gardens, cut telephone and telegraph wires, and burnt post boxes. One of the better known disobedients, Emily Davison, stepped in front of King George V's horse during the 1913 Epsom Derby and was fatally injured. These activists deliberately defied norms of civility in insisting that state institutions uphold their avowed commitment to protecting civil and political equality and see them as equal partners in the shared political project.[48]

To be clear, while arguments in favor of civil disobedience might be extended to justify certain acts of uncivil disobedience, these arguments do not offer a wholesale justification of uncivil disobedience. Such arguments could only justify certain types of uncivil disobedience undertaken in pursuit of goals that align with defenses of civil disobedience – including strengthening the rule of law, promoting democratic inclusion, and redressing injustice – or that align with the normative principles that ground political obligation.

In conclusion, the concept of uncivil disobedience is certainly not a short cut to legitimize protests and acts of resistance. It must be disaggregated for further evaluation, since different types call for different justifications. As will become clear in Part III, whether given acts of uncivil disobedience are permissible and justified might depend on many factors, including the agent's motivations and intended goals, the act's expected and actual consequences, and the constraints that the agents took upon themselves in order to minimize the risk of harm.

Sketching the normative dimensions of diverse types of uncivil disobedience is the task of Part III. First, Part II traces the resistant practices at the imagined origins of civil disobedience, the better to understand what civil and uncivil disobedience might consist of and hope to achieve.

---

[48] Delmas, 2018b.

Part II Practicing Disobedience

4 Thoreauvian Civil Resistance

On the evening of December 16, 1773, several dozen American colonists in Boston boarded three vessels operated by the British East India Company and dumped their cargo of tea into the harbor. The colonists, most of whom were members of the secret paramilitary political organization Sons of Liberty, were protesting the Tea Act approved by the British Parliament in May of that year. The law, which allowed the East India Company to sell Chinese tea in the American colonies without paying taxes, effectively created a monopoly for the company, seriously threatening the merchants of the American colonies.

At this point, colonial resistance had been building for the better part of a decade. The 1765 Stamp Act, which required colonists to pay taxes on printed materials, and the 1767 Townshend Acts, which regulated commerce and imposed additional taxes in the colonies, were seen as anathema to liberty: both laws, according to their critics, violated the colonists' constitutional right as British subjects because they were levied by a government over which the colonists had no control. Hence the famous rallying cry of "no taxation without representation," encapsulating the colonists' claim that they should be taxed only by their own representatives and not by a parliament in which they were not represented.[49] The Boston Tea Party, as the event became known, catalyzed colonial support for independence and contributed to the outbreak of the American Revolutionary War.

The Boston Tea Party is often seen as a foundational act of civil disobedience in the United States. Martin Luther King Jr. described it as a "massive act of civil disobedience" and situated the Civil Rights Movement's activism within this genealogy.[50] So did the conservative Tea Party movement of 2009–2016, which formed in opposition to the presidency of Barack Obama and paved the way for the ascent of Donald Trump. Assorted US far-right groups today also claim the lineage. For instance, adherents of the Last Sons of Liberty, a paramilitary organization that characterizes itself as an opponent of tyranny, partook in the January 6, 2021, attack on the US Capitol.

---

[49] The colonists had, in fact, refused the opportunity to elect their own representatives because they felt that doing so would lend the British Parliament legitimacy over the American colonies, even as their vote would be swamped by parliamentarians from metropolitan Britain. See Morgan (2012).

[50] King (2000, p. 96). King added the sentence, "In our own nation, the Boston Tea Party represented a massive act of civil disobedience," to the version of the "Letter from Birmingham Jail" that constitutes the fifth chapter of *Why We Can't Wait*. See Souza dos Santos (2024, chap. 3, especially pp. 131–133, and Appendix).

The Boston Tea Party does not satisfy the commonly accepted standards of civil disobedience. For one thing, the act wasn't suitably public, because the resisters snuck on board the vessels in the cover of darkness, many of them disguised as Mohawk warriors. Nor, of course, did the colonists give authorities advance notice of their planned action. The Sons of Liberty did immediately take responsibility for and defend the action, and notably they grounded their protest in a valid constitutional principle. However, the Boston Tea Party was not nonviolent. At a time when one could be hanged for destroying private property, the Sons of Liberty dumped 92,000 pounds of tea overboard, causing property damage worth £9,659, or $1.7 million in today's US dollars.

The Sons of Liberty were not trying to be civil disobedients. They defended their action as a revolt against an illegitimate government, not as a plea for Parliament to reconsider a couple of unfair taxes within an otherwise sufficiently just system. This tension between the Sons' avowedly revolutionary goals and the historical narrative presenting the Boston Tea Party as the original American act of civil disobedience invites us to scrutinize resistant practices from the perspectives of disobedients themselves and to see how their understandings of resistance complicate many of the stories we tell ourselves about civil and uncivil disobedience.

Part II sets out to examine disobedience from the standpoint of practitioner. I begin in this section with Henry David Thoreau's influential conception of civil resistance before turning to anarchist conceptions of direct action in Section 5 and, in Section 6, Mahatma Gandhi's and Martin Luther King's philosophies of nonviolence.

• • •

Three-quarter centuries after the Boston Tea Party, in nearby Concord, Massachusetts, Henry David Thoreau spent a night in jail for refusing to pay a state tax in protest against the institution of slavery, the extermination of Native Americans, and the war against Mexico. Thoreau is widely seen as another founding figure and paragon of civil disobedience, yet his principled tax refusal did not necessarily qualify as civil disobedience on the standard account.

Thoreau worked hard to justify his actions, however, delivering public lectures on the subject in 1848. In these lectures titled "The Rights and Duties of the Individual in Relation to Government," Thoreau justified his tax refusal as a practical and symbolic way to withdraw cooperation with the government and called on others to do the same. These lectures formed the basis of *Resistance to Civil Government*, which was published in 1849, revised in 1866, four years after Thoreau's death, and released under the title *Civil*

Disobedience.[51] The absence of any mention of "civil disobedience" in the text suggests the title wasn't Thoreau's, but scholars debate the matter, and the term remains commonly attributed to him.

Thoreau, like the Sons of Liberty, looms large in the social and political imaginary about both civil disobedience and insurrection. It is thus important to read his text attentively in order to guard against the misinterpretations he has been subjected to. This section covers Thoreau's scathing critique of obedience and his defense of the duty to disassociate from an unjust government. I also aim to correct the common misreading of Thoreau as concerned with the purity of his moral conscience and examine his incipient anarchism, which justifies his conception of resistance as noncooperation.

4.1 Against Obedience

The question at the heart of Thoreau's essay is this one: What obligations do subjects owe their civil government?[52] Thoreau takes as his foil the utilitarian and Christian philosopher William Paley, who defended a "duty of submission to civil government" or "duty of civil obedience" on the basis of "expediency" or utility. Thoreau responds that the demands of justice outweigh those of expediency, so that resistance is warranted when a government perpetuates grave injustice. The "civil" in Paley's "civil obedience" and Thoreau's "civil resistance" thus refers to the political relation between civilian subjects and their civil government. It has nothing to do with restraint, decorum, or any other behavioral norm.

Thoreau puts forth a radical critique of the idea that citizens are morally bound to submit to law, offering instead a stirring defense of their responsibility to resist injustice. His rebuttal of political obligation is grounded in the recognition of large gaps between law and justice:

> Law never made men a whit more just; and, by means of their respect for it, even the well-disposed are daily made the agents of injustice. A common and natural result of an undue respect for law is, that you may see a file of soldiers, colonel, captain, corporal, privates, powder-monkeys, and all, marching in admirable order over hill and dale to the wars, against their wills, ay, against their common sense and consciences, which makes it very steep marching indeed, and produces a palpitation of the heart.[53]

The state demands uncritical obedience and fosters in the public the opinion that obedience is a virtue. But what the state commands is often death and

---

[51] Thoreau, 1991.

[52] This section draws from my contribution to Çıdam, Scheuerman, Delmas et al. (2020).

[53] Thoreau (1991, p. 30).

destruction; in obeying, people take part in the perpetration of daily injustices and large-scale atrocities – in Thoreau's time, against Native Americans, Mexicans, and enslaved Africans and African-descended persons. More than a century later, Howard Zinn reminds us that "[h]istorically, the most terrible things – war, genocide, and slavery – have resulted not from disobedience but from obedience."[54]

The obedient not only feel morally bound to comply but also are relieved of any responsibility for the acts they are commanded to perform. Thoreau attacks these default attitudes by enjoining people to stop serving the state "as machines, with their bodies"[55] and by arguing that obedient citizens are complicit with the state's nefarious projects:

> It is not a man's duty, as a matter of course, to devote himself to the eradication of any, even the most enormous, wrong; he may still properly have other concerns to engage him; but it is his duty, at least, to wash his hands of it, and, if he gives it no thought longer, not to give it practically his support.[56]

Thoreau's answer to the question of political obligation is clear: subjects owe nothing to a state that creates and perpetuates grave injustice. Rather, their duty is to not contribute to the perpetration of serious wrongs.

4.2 Injustice and Conscience

Many scholars, Arendt and Rawls chief among them, have read Thoreau as principally concerned with the purity of his moral conscience. Rawls describes Thoreau's action as "conscientious refusal," lacking civil disobedience's appeal to the political community. Arendt likewise contends that Thoreau's resistance is not political, on her view because he acts alone rather than in concert with others.

Parts of Thoreau's essay support this individual- and conscience-centered reading of the duty to dissociate oneself from injustice. His claim that a citizen's duty is not to contest injustice but, less stringently, to not contribute to it is arguably an example. Thoreau also writes that "under the name of Order and Civil Government, we are all made at last to pay homage to and support our own meanness,"[57] further suggesting that what's wrong with habitual submission to an unjust state is the corruption of individual moral lives.

However, conscience-based appeals are not necessarily apolitical. In Thoreau's time, and indeed today, appeals to conscience are a common rhetorical ploy to political motivate action. Consider that Thoreau and his

---

[54] Zinn (2011, p. 420).   [55] Zinn (2011, p. 420).   [56] Thoreau (1991, p. 34).
[57] Thoreau (1991, p. 34).

contemporaries used similar strategies to urge more from complacent Abolitionists. "At most, they give only a cheap vote," Thoreau laments at one point in *Civil Disobedience* – a case of browbeating with obvious political valence.[58] Angelina Grimké, the feminist and Abolitionist daughter of a South Carolina enslaver, was another exponent of this genre, excoriating whites who were satisfied to denounce slavery from the distance of the North:

> The interests of the North, you must know, my friends, are very closely combined with those of the South. The Northern merchants and manufacturers are making their fortunes out of the produce of slave labour, the grocer is selling your rice and sugar; how then can these men bear a testimony against slavery without condemning themselves?[59]

For Abolitionists like Grimké and Thoreau, tracing citizens' complicity with horrors from which they felt distant was a consciousness-raising effort. These authors perceived that holding readers to account for their own moral failings might move them. This was not just a rhetorical manipulation, either. As Grimké explains in a letter to a friend, slavery fostered prejudice and thwarted compassion among southern white people, eroding their moral capacities and leaving them unable to cultivate Christian virtue. She cites the testimony of a born-again Abolitionist describing how living as a free white person under slave law had distorted his moral sense: "I had become so familiar with the loathsome features of slavery, that they *ceased to offend* – besides, I had become a *southern man* in all my feelings, and it is a part of our *creed* to defend slavery."[60]

Ultimately, I would argue that, if Thoreau emphasizes the moral injury suffered by citizens complicit with state injustice, he does so as a form of moral suasion. This is potentially an effective call to action – the mode whereby Thoreau encourages readers to *do* right. Thoreau's imperative – "I do not lend myself to the wrong which I condemn" – entails a demand to rectify injustice because the government acts in the citizen's name and derives its power from the citizen's cooperation. Obedience makes possible the state's continued wrongdoing and therefore amounts to acquiescence to, and responsibility for, what it does – no matter the nature of the government. Even under tyranny, individual submission fuels the state machine.

4.3 Noncooperation and Anarchy

How should citizens respond to the call to resist their unjust government? Disobedience is one way, according to Thoreau: "If [the injustice] is of such a nature that it requires you to be the agent of injustice to another, then, I say,

---

[58] Thoreau (1991, p. 33).   [59] Grimké, 1838.
[60] Grimké (2003, Letter VIII). Emphases in original.

break the law. Let your life be a counter-friction to stop the machine."[61] Thoreau's own disobedient actions suggest that such actions need not be civil (in the behavioral sense), public, or nonviolent. Thoreau participated in the Underground Railroad – a covert project – at great risk to himself. He also praised John Brown's 1859 raid on Harpers Ferry, a violent and ultimately unsuccessful action intended to initiate further violence in the form of an armed slave revolt.[62]

Crucially, Thoreau recognizes the need for collective action and appeals to the political community in his lectures and writings. His appeals are very different from those that Rawls and Arendt hear at the heart of civil disobedience, as he calls on all to cease cooperation with the government. Thoreau does not see his own tax resistance not as a "solitary" act, to use Arendt's word, but as a link in a long chain leading to revolution:

> If a thousand men were not to pay their tax bills this year, that would not be a violent and bloody measure, as it would be to pay them, and enable the State to commit violence and shed innocent blood. This is, in fact, the definition of a peaceable revolution, if any such is possible. If the tax gatherer, or any other public officer, asks me, as one has done, "But what shall I do?" my answer is, "If you really wish to do anything, resign your office." When the subject has refused allegiance, and the officer has resigned his office, then the revolution is accomplished.[63]

Noncooperation, even by a minority, starves the state machine, potentially bringing about transformative effects: "A minority is powerless while it conforms to the majority; ... but it is irresistible when it clogs by its whole weight."[64]

Thoreau's political philosophy proves to be anarchist at its core. As James Ingram persuasively argues, for Thoreau, "Rulers are not to be replaced, but left behind."[65] Contra readings of Thoreau as a "democrat"[66] or "constitutional patriot,"[67] Eraldo Souza dos Santos likewise argues that the horizon of Thoreau's political vision is the abolition of civil government.[68] Thoreauvian civil resistance – this original blueprint of civil disobedience – is radical indeed. Ingram even suggests that what Thoreau "proposes is not civil disobedience, but what anarchists term *direct action*: practices by which people, rather than petitioning the state, express their demands by disrupting social or official life."[69]

Is anarchist direct action, in fact, a blueprint for civil disobedience, or are these practices alien to each other – even opposed? The next section takes up this question.

---

[61] Thoreau (1991, p. 36).   [62] Thoreau, 2001.   [63] Thoreau (1991, p. 38).
[64] Thoreau (1991, p. 38).   [65] Ingram (2021, pp. 186–187).   [66] Laugier & Ogien, 2010.
[67] Habermas, 1985.   [68] Souza dos Santos (2024, chap. 1).   [69] Ingram (2021, p. 185).

5 Anarchist Direct Action

Activists and organizers engaged in civil disobedience commonly reference direct action and routinely treat it as interchangeable with civil disobedience. In his "Letter from a Birmingham Jail," for instance, King describes civil disobedient actions like sit-ins and marches as direct action. Responding to white moderates who question Civil Rights militancy, he asks, "Why direct action? Why sit-ins, marches, etc.? Isn't negotiation a better path?" King answers that the purpose of direct action is "to create such a crisis and establish such creative tension that a community that has constantly refused to negotiate is forced to confront the issue."[70] Thus he views civil disobedience or direct action as a kind of political accelerator, a means to petition authorities and force them to listen to the movement's grievances and demands. In contrast, Ingram considers petition the province of civil disobedience alone, whereas he views direct action as the strategic withdrawal from, and disabling of, the state.[71]

How should we make sense of the relationship between civil disobedience and direct action? This section approaches this question by examining anarchists' understanding of direct action as first and foremost an alternative to action via political processes.

5.1 What Direct Action Is Not

The concept of direct action arose in the late nineteenth and early twentieth centuries within revolutionary leftist organizations strewn across the globe, many associated with causes like syndicalism, which sought to make labor unions the owners of the means of production.[72] Labor organizers debated the meaning of direct action, its justification, and its role in class struggle, while opponents of the practice smeared it by association with violence, terrorism, and political assassination. As the American anarcho-feminist Voltairine de Cleyre wrote in 1912, detractors had flipped the concept of direct action "inside out, and upside down, and hindside before, and sideways, by occurrences out of the control of those who used the [expression] in their proper sense."[73]

What is the proper sense of direct action, then? It is most easily defined by what it is not: it is not political action, which anarchists also referred to as indirect action. For de Cleyre, indirect or political action consists in following the avenues set out by political institutions to bring about change. Under a representative or parliamentary government, the central avenue of political action is voting in

---

[70] King (1991, pp. 70–71).

[71] Ingram, 2021. Ingram views Thoreau as a paragon of an anarchist "politics of withdrawal" and Gandhi as exemplar of a "politics of community."

[72] See Scalmer (2023) for a transnational history of the concept.   [73] De Cleyre (2004, p. 47).

elections. In a 1903 pamphlet, the French anarchist-syndicalist Émile Pouget argues that direct action is the "rebuttal of democratism" or "negation of Parliamentarism."[74] On this view, whereas parliamentarism erects and legitimizes authority and demands obedience and passivity, direct action manifests workers' freedom and agency.

In her essay, de Cleyre rebuts those socialists who believe that "political action and political action only can win the workers' battle."[75] While opponents condemned direction action as "the author of mischief incalculable," de Cleyre defends it as doing significantly more good than harm, which she cannot say of indirect action. Her calculus here goes beyond the instrumentalist question of what strategy is most likely to bring about the revolution: de Cleyre believes the good of direct action also lies in its ability to foster in citizens the virtues that enable them to establish and maintain a free society – virtues that have no place in electoral politics.

In particular, de Cleyre argues that the injunction to channel grievances through the ballot entails that workers "be peaceable, industrious, law-abiding, patient" and not "rise up" even against obstacles to participation in political action itself, such as disenfranchisement. For to do so "might 'set back the [working-class] party.'" This mode of operating, she writes,

> destroys initiative, quenches the individual rebellious spirit, teaches people to rely on someone else to do for them what they should do for themselves; finally renders organic the anomalous idea that by massing supineness together until a majority is acquired, then through the peculiar magic of that majority, this supineness is to be transformed into energy.[76]

On de Cleyre's view, direct action is an antidote to the docility of political action and the only sustainable method to achieve emancipation. Similarly, Pouget highlights the value of direct action as a source of energy and "moral impregnation," for it releases workers "from the straitjacket of passivity" and fosters their "will-power," "sovereignty," and "continued growth."[77]

5.2 What Direct Action Is

Through direct action, workers actively put pressure on the boss and, beyond, on the state, to obtain the satisfaction of some demand. But exactly what form direct action takes is a matter of debate.

Pouget states that direct action is not any one thing – for instance, it can be "anodyne" or "very violent," depending on what the circumstances demand.[78] However Pouget's insistence that direct action is "the symbol of revolutionary

---

[74] Pouget (2003, p. 1).   [75] De Cleyre (2004, p. 58).   [76] De Cleyre (2004, p. 59).
[77] Pouget (2003, p. 5 and 19).   [78] Pouget (2003, p. 15).

unionism [i.e., syndicalism] in action" suggests that in his view the labor strike epitomizes the practice.

For her part, de Cleyre argues that "direct action has always been used, and has the historical sanction of the very people now reprobating it."[79] She illustrates this claim with reference to a number of historical instances of "peaceable" direct action: American colonists' non-importation agreements against the British; the Salvation Army's "singing, praying, and marching" for their freedom of assembly; the Industrial Workers' strikes for higher wages; New York housewives' butchery boycotts, seeking to lower the price of meat; Quakers' persistent refusal to pay taxes, take up arms, or swear allegiance to any government; and abolitionists' organization of the Underground Railroad. But de Cleyre does not consider violence disqualifying and also cites what she considers justified cases of "violent direct action," including the Boston Tea Party.

Indeed, de Cleyre underscores the violence inherent in strikes, which she considers legitimate direction action. A telegraph strike "means cutting wires and poles, and getting fake scabs in to spoil the instruments." A steel mill strike "means beating up the scabs, breaking the windows, setting the gauges wrong, and ruining the expensive rollers together with tons and tons of material." A garment workers' strike "means having an unaccountable fire, getting a volley of stones through an apparently inaccessible window, or possibly a brickbat on the manufacturer's own head. A strike in the building trades "means dynamited structures." And, in the case of any strike, "fights between strike-breakers and scabs against strikers and strike-sympathizers, between People and Police."[80]

As de Cleyre's analysis of strikes indicates, *sabotage* – the worker's attack on his work tool and product – is an important weapon in the arsenal of proletarian warfare. Pouget agrees, memorably describing "sabotage as a form of revolt . . . as old as human exploitation."[81] Sabotage epitomizes direct action and improves the chances that a strike will succeed: by destroying or disabling the work equipment, sabotage preempts the use of scabs and soldiers to keep the factory running. But sabotage doesn't end with the destruction of tools; Pouget details the many other forms that sabotage can take, including work stoppages and slowdowns; targeting production quality (e.g., cutting clothes according to the wrong patterns or providing a good product where the boss serves a bad one); "open-mouthed sabotage," meaning blowing the whistle on bosses' sordid business practices; and work-to-rule strike, which involves the worker's strict

---

[79] De Cleyre (2004, p. 50). Emphasis in original.   [80] De Cleyre (2004, p. 57).
[81] Pouget (1913, p. 38).

adherence to the rules of their work contract with the goal of disrupting and slowing down the work process.[82]

Certainly, neither Pouget nor de Cleyre would conflate direct action and civil disobedience as the latter is widely understood today. For them, direct action was a tactic specifically of class struggle, designed to counter a far more destructive enemy: while the proletarian sabotage "hits capital only in the bank account," Pouget writes, capital (itself a form of sabotage, in his view) "strikes at the sources of human life, ruins the health of the people and fills the hospitals and the cemeteries."[83] Still, proletarian sabotage and the labor strike more broadly *hit*. They aren't supposed to be civil. Sabotage is usually covert, and strikes tend to involve violence. The goal of direct action is not to communicate or persuade. It is to empower workers and leverage their collective power to coerce employers and industries – not only for better wages and working conditions but also, ultimately, to bring about the revolution: to destroy the imperium of capital and place the system of production in the hands of the workers.

5.3 Direct Action and Civil Disobedience

Insofar as de Cleyre wants to describe historical and contemporary cases of civil disobedience (loosely conceived, as we saw) as direct action, she is not especially interested in distinguishing the two concepts. But if we understand civil disobedience from a liberal or deliberative perspective – as an appeal to the majority on the basis of widely accepted constitutional principles – then we could highlight a contrast between the two, and summarize it in terms of deeds versus words. We could then associate civil disobedience with indirect action rather than direct action, given the civil disobedient act's function as a plea to legally constituted authorities.

Agents engaged in direct action do not rely on authorities; they rely only on themselves. "Every person who ever had a plan to do anything, and went and did it, or who laid his plan before others, and won their co-operation to do it with him, without going to external authorities to please do the thing for them," de Cleyre writes, "was a direct actionist."[84] David Graeber's conception of direct action and civil disobedience echoes de Cleyre's:

> [D]irect action is the insistence, when faced with structures of unjust authority, on acting as if one is already free. One does not solicit the state. One does not even necessarily make a grand gesture of defiance. Insofar as

---

[82] Jessica Bulman-Pozen and David Pozen (2015) conceive of work-to-rule strikes as cases of "uncivil obedience."

[83] Pouget (1913, p. 107).   [84] De Cleyre (2004, p. 48).

one is capable, one proceeds as if the state does not exist. This is the difference, in principle, between direct action and civil disobedience (though in practice there often is a good deal of overlap between the two). When one burns a draft card, one is withdrawing one's consent or cooperation from a structure of authority one deems illegitimate, but doing so is still a form of protest, a public act addressed at least partly to the authorities themselves. Typically, one practicing civil disobedience is also willing to accept the legal consequences of his actions. Direct action takes matters a step further. The direct actionist does not just refuse to pay taxes to support a militarized school system, she combines with others to try to create a new school system that operates on different principles. She proceeds as she would if the state did not exist and leaves it to the state's representatives to decide whether to try to send armed men to stop her.[85]

If civil disobedience is first and foremost a mode of address, "a form of protest, a public act addressed at least partly to the authorities themselves," direct action is a mode of doing undertaken "as if the state does not exist." It is a form of defiance that has no interest in communicating with the entity defied but rather circumvents it, and seeks to bring about change by cultivating free and caring forms of community in the here and now.

Benjamin Franks distinguishes civil disobedience and direct action along three dimensions.[86] First, civil disobedients, but not direct actionists, commit to nonviolence. Second, civil disobedients necessarily break laws, whereas direct action is not necessarily illegal, as when it takes the form of open-mouthed sabotage or work-to-rule strike. Third, and crucially, direct action is *prefigurative*. Prefiguration, a hallmark of anarchist ethics, holds that "the means have to be in accordance with the ends" – that is, the method of action must mirror or prefigure the goal that is sought. In practice, this means that anarchist acts of resistance, including direct action, should manifest desiderata like self-reliance, mutual aid, and free agreement. It is, for instance, on the basis of prefiguration that anarchists critique Marxist-Leninist avant-garde politics, which demands deference to party leaders and leads to the abdication of individual responsibility.[87] Civil disobedience, for its part, has no intrinsic relationship with prefiguration. It may be justified instrumentally, by its beneficial effects alone.

•••

While the classical Anarchist revolutionary tradition has receded from the political scene, "neo-anarchism" or "small-a anarchism," understood as an anti-oppression and non-hierarchical organizing framework infuses a large

---

[85] Graeber (2009, p. 203).   [86] Franks (2003, pp. 17–18).   [87] Bakunin, 1990.

number of left-wing social movements today.[88] Informed and experimented with since the 1970s by peace activists, feminist and queer groups, and radical environmental activists, neo-anarchism was turbocharged by the alter-globalization movement of the late 1990s, the Argentinian uprising of 2001, anti-austerity movements in Europe, and Occupy Wall Street. Horizontalism – the creation of organizational structures that are non-hierarchical, decentralized, and participatory, where all members have an equal voice and decision-making power – is a key component of prefiguration.[89] Horizontalist groups coordinate activity and strategy through general assemblies, and seek consensus in their decision-making. They reclaim public spaces where they establish protest encampments which sometimes turn into police-free "temporary autonomous zones" (a term popularized by anarchist Hakim Bey).[90] Black Lives Matter embraces both prefigurative politics and horizontalism, but not anarchism itself.[91] Mohandas Gandhi and Martin Luther King, Jr., to whom we now turn, embraced prefiguration.

6 Decolonial Nonviolence

Mohandas Karamchand Gandhi and Martin Luther King, Jr., are central figures in the pantheon of civil disobedience. Both saw themselves as Thoreau's heirs and embraced the ethic and politic of prefiguration. Yet each also departs from Thoreauvian and anarchist resistance by rejecting violence. This section examines their respective philosophies of nonviolence, correcting the misperception that they were moral absolutists with respect to nonviolence. I also push back on the romantic narrative of the Civil Rights Movement, which distorts and sanitizes practices of civil disobedience.

6.1 Gandhi's *Satyagraha*

Gandhi, the most influential figure in India's campaign for independence from British rule, developed and conceptualized a practice and philosophy of nonviolence he termed *satyāgraha*. Literally "truth-force" in Sanskrit, this neologism designated the nonviolent resistance Gandhi began experimenting with while working as a lawyer in South Africa. There, Gandhi led a multiethnic movement against discriminatory legislation targeting Indians, Africans, and Coloreds (multiracial South Africans). He perfected this nonviolent resistant practice in India, organizing a broad noncooperation movement, which aimed to paralyze

---

[88] Graeber, 2009.

[89] Argentinian activists coined the term (*horizontalidad*) to describe the dynamic self-management of such non-hierarchical social relations. See Sitrin (2012).

[90] Bey, 2003.   [91] Woodly, 2021.

British governance through mass boycotts of British goods and services, withdrawals and resignations from British institutions, and tax refusals.

Gandhi sought to distinguish his form of resistance, which he described as "dynamic," from the pacificism theorized by the Russian novelist Leo Tolstoy and practiced elsewhere in the United Kingdom and South Africa.[92] At the heart of satyagraha is love and discipline. Gandhi's followers, *satyagrahis*, pledged themselves to nonviolence and swore their preparedness to suffer for the truth. "A satyāgrahi was ever ready to endure suffering and ever lays down his life to demonstrate to the world the integrity of his purpose and the justice of his demands," Gandhi said in a speech on March 7, 1919.

This preparedness to bear pain and suffer further distinguishes *satyagraha* from political violence:

> On the political field, the struggle on behalf of the people mostly consists in opposing error in the shape of unjust laws. When you have failed to bring the error home to the law-giver by way of petitions and the like, the only remedy open to you, if you do not wish to submit to error, is to compel him by physical force to yield to you or by suffering in your own person by inviting the penalty for the breach of the law. Hence *satyāgraha* largely appears to the public as Civil Disobedience or Civil Resistance. It is civil in the sense that it is not criminal.[93]

On Gandhi's view, an unjust law is an "error" and a lie, submission to which cannot ever be morally required. Gandhi sees two possible roads toward emancipation, once legal avenues of bringing about change have been exhausted: either political violence, which involves the use of physical force to coerce opponents, or *satyagraha*, which involves civilly disobeying the unjust law since it consists of "suffering in your own person by inviting the penalty for the breach of the law." Nonviolence is a compelling force (like physical violence) – but a spiritual one, wielded to persuade, not coerce, the opponent. Satyagraha is thus Gandhi's answer to unjust law.

In fact, the self-sacrifice required of satyāgrahi exceeds acceptance of legal penalties. It demands self-examination and self-purification – an extensive process usually involving prayer and fast to spiritually prepare oneself for "the pitting of one's whole soul against the will of the tyrant."[94] Satyagraha also demands "suffering wrong without retaliation," whether the brutality of police, soldiers, and other "evil-doers" (for instance, the security services hired by factory bosses) or the resistance of one's peers.[95]

Come what may, then, the satyagrahi renounces any right to self-defense. As Karuna Mantena has shown, Gandhi deems violence in individual and

---

[92] Gandhi (1973, p. 40).   [93] Gandhi (1973, p. 67).   [94] Gandhi (1973, p. 48).
[95] Gandhi (1973, p. 56).

collective self-defense not so much morally impermissible as futile.[96] Violence against colonial domination would cultivate the wrong kind of independence for India and breed the wrong kind of polity, amounting to a mere change of the personnel ruling a violent state that generates unstable conditions. Nonviolence is superior because only it can preserve the conditions enabling peace and concord after the decolonization struggle. "We reap exactly as we sow," Gandhi writes in *Hind Swaraj*, stressing an organic, prefigurative connection between means and ends at the heart of political action.[97] Nonviolence bolsters activists' sense of self-worth and dignity and enables them to affirm their agency and powers of self-determination even under conditions of political subjugation.

What is more, nonviolence proves to be a highly effective tactic of moral suasion. Richard Gregg, who introduced Gandhi's philosophy of nonviolence to the US public in 1934 through his monograph *The Power of Nonviolence*, argued that nonviolence ignites an affective and psychological chain reaction in the bystander and the opposition. This process begins with surprise at the defeat of one's expectation that activists will respond violently to their own violent repression. Surprise leads to wonder, followed by self-reflection, admiration for the activist and shame at one's conduct, and finally conversion. Gregg describes this process as "moral jiu-jitsu" because the opponent loses their balance and experiences a profound disorientation, as if the world was turned upside down – the strong is revealed weak and the weak as strong.[98] That is the power of nonviolence.

6.2 King's Nonviolent Direct Action

King was deeply influenced by Gandhi's analysis of the power of nonviolence. He wrote a Foreword to the second edition of Gregg's book in 1959, which had been updated with the examples of nonviolent (overt and covert) resistance against the Nazis in Europe and of the 1955–1956 Montgomery Bus Boycott in Alabama. King praised the book, wishing it "a wide readership, particularly among those, in this country and throughout the world, who are seeking ways of achieving full social, personal and political freedom in a manner consistent with human dignity."[99]

Mantena identifies in King's writings and speeches (as in Gandhi's) his endorsement of what she dubs the "three faces of nonviolence": morally, nonviolence is the right means by which oppressed people can regain dignity and self-respect; strategically, it is a necessary means to just and stable political

---

[96] Mantena, 2012.   [97] Gandhi (1909, chap. 16).   [98] Gregg (1960, chap. 2).
[99] King in Gregg (1960, p. 9).

results and future democratic concord; and tactically, the dramatization of nonviolent actors' discipline works effectively to persuade opponents.[100] Like Gandhi, King rejected violence on pragmatic grounds, as futile and counterproductive in light of post-struggle aspirations for democratic concord and racial integration.

But King recognized the legitimacy of Black anger in response to police brutality, racial discrimination, and poverty; and this anger frequently erupted in civil unrest, especially in what is known as the "long, hot summer" of 1967, when over 150 riots took place. As Brandon Terry highlights, "King argued that it was best, both politically and for one's own flourishing, to channel anger into less corrosive emotions."[101] Rage makes one powerless. Anger should instead be directed into creative nonviolence, cleansed from its violent and vengeful impulses while retaining its lucid assessment of and indignation at white supremacy. Nonviolence is, for King, an "ethic of love" built on Christian *agape* – a kind of love for humanity which "enjoins us to see even our political *enemies* as moral equals whom we are interdependent with and vulnerable to, and whose needs and welfare we are obligated to consider."[102] Nonviolence imagines a different future.

King also located the transformative power of nonviolence in the activist's steadfast courage and preparedness to self-sacrifice. For King, nonviolent activists must not only "willingly accept the penalty of imprisonment in order to arouse the conscience of the community over its injustice," as he wrote in the "Letter from a Birmingham Jail," but they must also "accept blows without retaliating."[103] Nonviolent activists display "unearned suffering" as they absorb and reflect, rather than defending themselves against, state and mob violence.[104] In doing so, they make the reality of their own oppression stark, compelling the white majority to see it and renounce it out of shame at their contribution to its maintenance.

King, but not Gandhi, deemed nonviolence compatible with coercion. After the Montgomery bus boycott, which unleashed spectacular white retaliatory violence, King saw appeals to conscience as insufficient. He wrote about the campaign in Birmingham, Alabama, which involved a mass boycott of local businesses, sit-ins and marches, including by youth participants in the Children's Crusade: "Nonviolent direct action seeks to create such a crisis and establish such creative tension that a community that has constantly refused to negotiate is forced to confront the issue."[105] King, however, does not name coercion in the letter, equivocating about what Alexander Livingston dubs "the coercive face of nonviolence" until 1966, when the Civil Rights Movement,

---

[100] Mantena, 2018.   [101] Terry (2018, p. 24).   [102] Terry (2018, pp. 23–24).
[103] King (1991, p. 70).   [104] King, 1960.   [105] King (1991, p. 71).

having formally ended the southern racial caste system, pivoted the struggle for equality toward northern ghettos.[106] It then became clear that nonviolent resistance, to succeed, needed not only to arouse and persuade but also to disrupt and confront, by means of "some form of constructive coercive power."[107]

As Livingston shows, King's philosophy of nonviolence and civil disobedience evolved over time. Early on, in the "Letter," King both proclaims nonviolent activists' aim to "arouse the conscience of the [white] majority" and appeals to the United States government's federal authority and to the principles of political morality entrenched in the Constitution, presenting nonviolent discipline as evidence of activists' embrace of these principles. (The "highest respect for law" he professes, however, must be understood as directed toward natural law, not positive law.[108]) But these appeals to white conscience and to constitutional principles fade out of his late theory of civil disobedience, to make place for "militant love" – "a militant conception of protest politics that looks toward emancipatory transformation beyond the terms of the nation's constitutional frame."[109] In *Where Do We Go from Here?*, King describes as a "miscalculation" civil rights leaders' assumption that "without massive upheavals certain systemic changes were inevitable as the whole nation reexamined and searched its conscience," given the realization that white Americans' power was "conscienceless."[110] Stokely Carmichael (later Kwame Ture) had put the problem succinctly years earlier: "in order for nonviolence to work, your opponent must have a conscience. The United States has none."[111] Appeals to shame and denunciations of hypocrisy would not work.

The problem runs deep, as Livingston's insightful analysis shows, for King "denies that there is any common moral language shared between white and black Americans ... The work of liberatory integration is therefore in no small part the creation of new values that could serve as the shared language of any future association worth fighting for."[112] Nonviolence must not only force negotiations and dismantle unjust institutions; it must also imagine and bring about a new language through which the work of rebuilding could be done, collectively.

6.3 Myth and Reality

The consensus narrative of the Civil Rights Movement has simplified, sanitized, and distorted King's rich philosophy of nonviolence and ignored the complex

---

[106] Livingston (2020, p. 704).   [107] King (2010, p. 137).   [108] King (1991, p. 74).
[109] Livingston (2020, p. 711).   [110] King (2010, pp. 20, 38).
[111] Carmichael's speech is featured in Göran Olsson's film *The Black Power Mixtape 1967–1975* (2011).
[112] Livingston (2020, pp. 711–712).

battle of ideas waged within the movement about nonviolence itself. Consensus history suggests that the Civil Rights Movement achieved major goals through nonviolence alone, thereby sidelining the roles of radical activists and groups, including Black nationalists. To the extent that King's Southern Christian Leadership Conference was successful, this was in part due to the contrast it made with Black Power groups, which made King and his allies seem moderate.

Furthermore, while civil rights activists are to be praised for their extraordinary sacrifices, in celebrating their absorption of violence, the consensus narrative erects nonviolence into a normative imperative, thereby assuming the state's legitimacy even amid state-authored and state-sanctioned violence and at least implicitly condemning those Black Americans who did try to defend themselves. Consider the experience of Angela Davis, who grew up amid white racial terror in Birmingham. Her neighborhood saw such a constant stream of bombings of Black homes that it soon became known as Dynamite Hill. The city itself was nicknamed "Bombingham." She writes in her autobiography:

> Every so often a courageous Black family moved or built on the white side of Center Street [the city's color line], and the simmering resentment erupted in explosions and fires. On a few such occasions, Police Chief Bull Connor would announce on the radio that a "n–r family" had moved on the white side of the street. His prediction "There will be bloodshed tonight" would be followed by a bombing. So common were the bombings on Dynamite Hill that the horror of them diminished.[113]

Davis's analysis underscores both the prevalence of racial terror and the state's encouragement and commission of violence against Blacks.

The romanticized history of the Black freedom struggle ends up serving the status quo by misrepresenting nonviolent activists' practices and fostering a kind of optimism about the possibility of US racial justice that is unmoored from reality, as Juliet Hooker has shown.[114] Erin Pineda, too, has debunked such myths, which seem to be manufactured for the purpose of preserving and justifying an oppressive state.[115] She has revealed, through archival research, civil rights activists' own understanding of their civil disobedience as "decolonizing praxis." Uncovering a global network of freedom struggle, Pineda shows that activists in the Civil Rights Movement saw themselves as militants against colonialism and imperialism, linking the domestic to the international – the Indian independence movement to the "occupied territory" of Black America.[116]

---

[113] Davis (1974, p. 95). My redaction.   [114] Hooker (2023, p. 101).   [115] Pineda, 2021a.
[116] Pineda, 2021a; Baldwin, 1966.

Finally, against the popular understanding of Civil Rights activists being absolutely committed to nonviolence, most organizers and activists throughout the country, but especially in the Jim Crow south, carried weapons to defend themselves from white violence. Carmichael, who served as the chairman of the Student Nonviolent Coordination Committee, estimated that 90 percent of SNCC's field workers were armed. Like fellow civil rights leaders Robert F. Williams and Charles E. Cobb Jr., and Black nationalist Akinyele Umoja, Carmichael considered armed self-defense necessary for the operation of non-violent activities like boycotts, marches, and voting registration.[117] Even King kept guns in his home for protection. He argued that arms shouldn't be visible at demonstrations, because armed self-defense had no chance of gaining sympathetic white allies, without whom there could be no victory for the movement. But he did not consider self-defense illegitimate.

In short, the pantheon of civil disobedience misrepresents its own heroes. Gandhi and King did not consider nonviolence a moral necessity; they defended it on pragmatic grounds, given their respective goals of Indian self-rule and racial equality. Nor did civil rights activists and satyāgrahis seek to vindicate the state's promise of justice: as decolonial movements, both sought fundamental transformation of the constitutional order. The consensus narrative of the Civil Rights Movement defangs the transformative power of nonviolence as a decolonial praxis, turning it into a normative imperative that obfuscates state violence and undermines justifications of armed self-defense.

If even Gandhi's and King's nonviolence are more complicated – more provisional – than admirers of civil disobedience credit, what does this mean for the justifiability of violent and uncivil resistance? Part III brings us face to face with this central moral concern.

---

[117] Williams, 1998; Umoja, 2013; Cobb, 2014.

Part III Justifying Uncivil Disobedience

7 Violence

Consider the following scenes and actions.

In 1963, Thich Quang Duc immolated himself in South Vietnam to protest the Catholic government's persecution of Buddhists. Five more Buddhist monks and nuns immolated themselves that year.

In 1978–1980, Irish Republican Army (IRA) fighters imprisoned at Long Kesh and Armagh Women's Prison in Northern Ireland refused to wash and smeared the walls of their cells with bodily waste to protest the British government's revocation of their Special Category Status, which had provided them with many of the privileges of prisoners-of-war enunciated in the Geneva Conventions. The Dirty Protest, as it was known, was escalated with a hunger strike in 1981. Ten of the prisoners, including strike leader Bobby Sands, died.

In 2005, riots erupted in the suburbs (*banlieues*) of Paris and other French cities after two youths who hid in an electrical substation to avoid police interrogation died from electrocution. Rioters burned cars and public buildings, looted shops, and attacked civilians, police, and firefighters causing three deaths and many injuries.

In 2019–2020, hundreds of thousands of people marched peacefully in the streets of Hong Kong to demand democratic control over their affairs. Some frontline participants, however, used defensive force. Organizing to protect the mass of protesters from police violence and arrest, they dug up pavement, which they used to assemble roadblocks to slow down police vehicles. When police fired tear gas, the frontliners, wearing heat-resistant gloves, grabbed the canisters and threw them back at the police. They also threw Molotov cocktails and rocks.

In the aftermath of the police killing of George Floyd in Minneapolis in 2020, activists organized under the heading of Black Lives Matter took down Confederate flags and toppled Confederate monuments throughout the former Jim Crow states, from Oklahoma to Florida. All over the world, monuments celebrating historical figures responsible for slavery and colonization were vandalized and torn down.

Since 2021, the French environmental grassroots group Les Soulèvements de la Terre (Earth Uprisings) has occupied the sites of, and resorted to sabotage against, such environmentally destructive and extractive industries as cement production, oil and gas transportation, and agribusinesses.

Collectively, these cases raise questions about what constitutes violence and whether violence of particular sorts can constitute justified resistance. The banlieues riots featured clear cases of violence: harmful use of force against persons. But the others are not so easily classified. Does violence include harm to oneself, property destruction, or defensive use of force? Under what circumstances can these types of acts be justified, whether or not they count as violence?

7.1 Conceptual Foundations of Violence

There are high stakes involved in defining acts as violent: observers tend to condemn violent protests and excuse their repression, while nonviolent protests are more likely to win over allies. However, the designation of a protest as either violent or nonviolent is not a straightforward matter. Objective facts do not alone determine whether a given observer perceives resistance as violent.

Designations of violence and peacefulness occur within a preexisting frame of reference, based on diverse cultural understandings of what constitutes violence. Observers' determinations will also be influenced by their biases concerning resisters and their motives. And crucially, unless one is a direct participant in or eyewitness to an action, one will be exposed to it via media coverage. The press often does the labeling for us, describing protests as either violent or nonviolent according to criteria that may be ambiguous, unfair, and unstated. Such labels can make or break a protest movement: as social scientific research has shown, mainstream news coverage frequently delegitimizes protests by labeling them as violent.[118]

Even in the absence of observer bias, the binary opposition between violence and nonviolence is conceptually problematic, for it implies that acts of resistance fall neatly into one or the other category. But if violence is understood as the intentional and direct infliction of injury or harm, and nonviolence as the deliberate refraining from the use of force against persons, then we are left to contend with large gray areas. What about deliberately causing injury to oneself, as the Buddhist and IRA protesters did? What about coercion, unrelated to physical harm? Recall that Gandhi and liberal theorists view coercion as impermissible violence, whereas King and radical democrats consider coercion compatible with nonviolence.

Practitioners and theorists of civil disobedience often classify the hunger strike, which involves self-starvation, as a quintessentially nonviolent and noncoercive tactic. Yet this tactic is often seen as "political blackmail," and both the British and the Irish saw the IRA's hunger strike as coercive.[119] The World Health Organization considers self-harm violent, defining violence as "the intentional use of physical force or power, threatened or actual, *against oneself,* another person, or against a group or community, that either results in or

---

[118] Kilgo, 2021.   [119] See Delmas (2024).

has a high likelihood of resulting in injury, death, psychological harm, mal-development, or deprivation."[120] According to this definition, starving oneself, immolating oneself, or endangering one's bodily health through self-neglect, as in the Dirty Protest, are all acts of violence.

For his part, Gandhi believed that self-immolation and total fasting could accord with the principle of nonviolence if the agent harbored the right mental state – accessible to only a true satyagrahi, who has engaged in deep self-purification. He thus contrasted sātyagrahi fasts with the Irish republicans' hunger strikes, viewing the former as persuasive and the latter as coercive. Meanwhile, in a letter to Dr. King, Thich Nhat Hanh explained that Thich Quang Duc's self-immolation expressed "will and determination" and should be contrasted with suicide: "To express will by burning oneself, is not to commit an act of destruction but perform an act of construction, that is, to suffer and to die for the sake of one's people."[121]

As for property damage, it is often treated as a kind of violence, especially in Western societies founded upon liberal traditions, which see private property as an extension of personhood.[122] However, some societies (like France) are more tolerant of property damage and open to its compatibility with nonviolence than others, as we saw in Section 3 (although France has since increasingly aligned itself with neoliberal and repressive trends). Many practitioners count some types of property damage as nonviolent. For instance, members of the radical Catholic pacifist Plowshares movement deliberately damaged lethal objects such as nuclear weapons. In a 1968 action, the Catonsville Nine, before they founded Plowshares, burned 378 draft files with homemade napalm, targeting the administrative bureaucracy of war. These activists would not condone the destruction of life-sustaining property, such as habitation or medi-cation. But, as the activists saw it, the philosophy of nonviolence permitted the elimination of life-destroying property, to ensure respect for the dignity of human life.

My own view is that it is most useful to conceptualize property damage and self-harm as categorically distinct from both violence and nonviolence, to better recognize the ways in which property damage and self-harm mix features of violence and nonviolence while fully fitting neither. In any case, the important question is that of normatively assessing violence, property damage, and self-violence. To address that sort of question, theorists have deployed the theoret-ical framework of the ethics of self-defense.

---

[120] Krug et al., 2002, my emphasis.   [121] Nhat Hanh (2022, p. 148).

[122] Fortas (1968, pp. 48–49, 123–126); Smith (2013, pp. 3, 33).

7.2 Normative Justifications for the Use of Force

7.2.1 Defensive Violence

The ethics of defensive action are grounded in large part in the conviction that persons possess a fundamental and inalienable right to self-defense, making the use of force to defend oneself or others from an unjust attack a paradigmatic case of justified action. But many questions follow from this seemingly simple claim.

Can I permissibly defend myself from a pinch by punching my assailant? Can I kill a thief trying to steal my property? And who, exactly, is liable to be harmed in self-defense? Say a person is a victim of domestic abuse: Is she engaged in self-defense if she neutralizes her abuser while he is sleeping? Do I exercise a right to self-defense when I strike against a perceived threat that has not materialized? And do I have a right to defend myself from a just attack?

Ethicists have responded to such questions by developing a theoretical framework for the ethics of defensive action. This framework articulates requirements by which an agent must abide in order that the defensive harm they inflict be justified. Accounts of justified self-defense can be highly nuanced, but any such framework has two key elements: necessity and proportionality.

The necessity criterion holds that a defender must choose a course of action that inflicts the least harm necessary to defend against the threat. This assessment involves comparing the harm inflicted in self-defense with the harm that would be generated by alternative courses of action – including inaction, whereby the threatened person absorbs the threatened harm.[123] To effect this comparison, we need further to assess (a) the expected efficacy of the course of action chosen, that is, the likelihood of success in averting the attack, as well as (b) the expected risks, or the likelihood that the defensive act will cause other harms beyond those necessary to prevent an attack, such as harms to innocent third parties. All of these determinations are forward-looking: they must be made before engaging in defensive action. As a result, there are serious epistemic obstacles to evaluations of necessity. With this in mind, some scholars suggest that we look to the evidence available to the defender, rather than to the objective facts, which may not be accessible. For Helen Frowe, a person who reasonably, but mistakenly, believes her life is threatened can be permitted to use force in self-defense.[124]

The proportionality criterion differs from the necessity criterion in a subtle but important way. Where necessity requires that defensive action be the least harmful action among all of the alternatives, proportionality compares the harm

---

[123] Lazar, 2012.   [124] Frowe, 2010.

caused by the defender's action with that which she would suffer were she not to act. The criterion of proportionality thus asks us to assess the seriousness of the defensive harm, as compared with that of the harm being defended against. Proportionality, however, is not just a matter of neutrally comparing the harm the defender would suffer with the harm she causes to her assailant. If it were, then the moral positions of the assailant and the defender would be equal, and the rape victim who kills her attacker could be found to have used disproportionate force. But we can vindicate our common intuition that she is entitled to defend herself in this way by noting that her bodily integrity should count more than her abuser's life. The harm to the assailant caused by a defender can be morally "discounted," because the attacker is in the wrong – either they caused or are complicit in, or responsible for, a wrongful threat – and are therefore liable to defensive harms.[125] The more culpable an aggressor is, the more liable they are to defensive harm and the greater the moral discount to which the defender is entitled.

Did the Hong Kong protesters' use of force against police qualify as justified defensive harm? According to the theoretical framework just sketched, the protesters' use of force could be justified to the extent that it was necessary to avert a threat and proportionate to the seriousness of the threat. For instance, insofar as digging up the pavement to set up barricades, in fact, slowed down police vehicles and gave demonstrators time to evade wrongful arrest, the damage done to public property could well be justified. Countering police with their own tear gas could also be necessary and proportionate to defensive harm. However, some frontline protesters instead doused tear gas canisters with water, which they funneled into the canisters using traffic cones – a method that effectively neutralized this particular use of violence by police. Perhaps it follows that throwing the tear gas canisters back at the police was not necessary after all and therefore was not justified – at least among those who had traffic cones and water at hand – unless the case can further be made that this tactic posed less risks to protesters and bystanders than the neutralization tactic and/or brought additional benefits, such as police retreat.

Hong Kong protesters also threw rocks, flaming arrows, and Molotov cocktails at police. Was this justified use of defensive force? There is good reason to think that their acts protected peaceful demonstrators from police brutality and arrest and prevented the police from stopping the mass movement in its tracks. Yet these actions also led to an escalation of police violence. When the democracy movement was defeated, its violent acts became a justification for mass

---

[125] See Lazar (2012) on morally weighted harms; Frowe and Parry (2022) for an overview on the grounds for liability.

arrests and tightened legislation against dissent. Given China's history of harshly repressing protests in Hong Kong, these outcomes could have been expected. Should we then conclude that protesters' defensive use of force did not inflict the least necessary harm, given the likelihood that it would bring about other serious harms and the very low likelihood that the protest would succeed in achieving its aims?

We find ourselves confronting a dilemma, one that is especially acute in oppressive contexts. On the one hand, the more powerful, violent, and vengeful the aggressor (the state), the harder it is for defenders (protesters) to meet the necessity test. On the other hand, the permissibility of protest against oppression is intuitively obvious, even where such protests may be futile. Rather than concluding that necessity is not required to justify defensive force, some philosophers like Frowe have attempted to resolve this dilemma by affirming that victims may permissibly act to defend against threats to their honor or dignity.[126]

Kimberly Kessler Ferzan has objected that futile defensive harm of this kind was not defensive but expressive: it does not avert a threat to honor but it "expresses honor."[127] The advantage of recasting honor defense as expressive is further to explain why the defender may permissibly impose more harm than strictly necessary, namely, for the sake of a greater expressive value. Edmund Tweedy Flanigan also argues that those engaged in acts of futile resistance are not trying to defend themselves but trying to protest their victimization. In such cases, the harms they inflict are justified not because they avert a threat but because they are fitting expressions of rejection of the wrong done to them and fitting responses to the circumstances making it so that their resistance is futile.[128]

Avia Pasternak has also taken up the challenge of justifying the use of force by protesters, such as occurred during the 2005 French *banlieues* riots.[129] In her view, even harms that do not directly respond to threats to life and bodily integrity, but are instead initiated by protesters, can be justified as defense against serious and entrenched injustices. Drawing on social scientific research, she shows that most of those who take part in violent protests are motivated by a range of political goals: "bringing about policy change; expressing anger of existing policies and defiance of the state's authority; holding police officers accountable for their actions; and resisting their demo-cratic marginalization."[130] On this basis, she characterizes the harms violent

---

[126] Frowe (2014, chap. 4).   [127] Kessler Ferzan, 2018.   [128] Flanigan, 2023.
[129] Pasternak (2025, chap. 2).   [130] Pasternak (2025, p. 23).

protesters inflict not as "defensive" but as "protective," to mark actors' aim of protecting oppressed citizens' basic interests.[131]

Pasternak further argues that some of the (nonlethal) violence that protestors inflict on police and fellow citizens, and the damage they cause to public and private property, can meet the necessity and proportionality tests. First, she shows that violent protests can meet the necessity criterion insofar as protesters are marginalized and often ghettoized citizens with little or no access to either institutional channels of redress or peaceful forms of protest such as civil disobedience. She also underlines the high moral costs of inaction, which contributes to the indignity of the oppressed. In addition, Pasternak gives empirical reasons to credit the effectiveness of violent protests to deliver on their goal of communicating and expressing anger and defiance and achieve long-term policy change, suggesting a presumptively sufficient probability of success. Second, she assesses proportionality through a close examination of state personnel's and citizens' liability to defensive harm (inflicted on their person or property), based on police officers' role-related obligations and ordinary citizens' entanglement with injustice.[132]

7.2.2 (Non-)defensive Property Damage

Although Pasternak does not directly discuss the vandalizing and removal of Confederate monuments, her framework can be applied to justify the latter acts as "protective" uses of force against state threats to Black people's equal civil standing and right to safety. Other scholars have come up with different approaches to justify this type of public property damage.

Chong-Ming Lim conceives of political vandalism as a fitting response to tainted monuments, because the protest is especially effective in repudiating the white-supremacist messages embedded in the monuments. Alternatives, such as removing the monuments or preserving them in place alongside some sort of explanatory or disclamatory document such as a plaque, are, according to Lim, less expressively successful than defacing the monuments.[133] For his part, Ten-Herng Lai argues that tainted public commemorations are state-sponsored hate speech, so that vandalizing such commemoration is at least sometimes counter-speech fit for "blocking" and "undoing" the harms of hateful political symbols.[134]

William Scheuerman similarly classifies political vandalism in the category of symbolic politically motivated property destruction, thereby underscoring its communicative nature. The other categories in his typology include disruptive

---

[131] For a different theoretical approach to riots, see Havercroft (2021).
[132] Pasternak (2025, chap. 3–5).   [133] Lim, 2020.   [134] Lai, 2020.

property destruction – as in sabotage and environmental direct action – and the seizing of property, such as looting and "robinhoodism."[135] The key question when it comes to assessing such acts is their relation to violence against persons. Scheuerman argues that symbolic property destruction is the most readily justifiable from this perspective, and even potentially congruent with political nonviolence, whereas disruptive property damage and seizing property can be justified only on the basis of more demanding tests. In both cases, agents' "endeavors should typically represent a last resort that is suitably constrained, discriminating, and proportionate, with any tangible threats to human life reduced and, ideally, eliminated."[136]

The criteria of the defensive action framework thus resurface here. Andreas Malm, too, resorts to these criteria in defending disruptive property damage. In *How to Sabotage a Pipeline* he argues that radical environmental activism targeting property is permissible as a last resort given that peaceful mass protest has not produced the reforms necessary to preserve life in the face of climate change. Malm specifically defends certain acts of sabotage directed at affluent citizens of wealthy countries, for instance deflating the tires of sport-utility vehicles, which are some of the most popular polluting automobiles. Malm suggests that the affluent are fit targets because, unlike poor citizens who are ignored by governments, they have the capacity to exert pressure on officials.[137]

Les Soulèvements de la Terre (SLT), a French collective of environmentalist groups, farmers, trade unions, and others, defends sabotage to fight what they see as the government's inaction in the face of global warming and support for land and water privatization. Many SLT activists previously participated in the peaceful protests of Extinction Rebellion but felt frustrated by the movement's use of roadblocks and square occupation – tactics that inconvenience and alienate the public without clearly addressing the purported targets, namely government leaders and captains of industry. Instead, SLT targets for disruption those entities responsible for environmental destruction: a ski resort that seeks to create a reservoir of artificial snow, a conglomerate building a new airport on farmland, an agribusiness constructing a mega-basin (huge private water reserve), fossil fuel companies.

For instance, in 2022, 200 SLT activists invaded a cement plant whose owner was trying to expand its quarries. The activists cut cables, spilled bags of cement, damaged construction equipment, smashed windows, and tagged walls with graffiti. The event attracted media attention, which is one of SLT's goals: to speak to the public about the French government's culpability in permitting and encouraging environmentally destructive projects. The act of

---

[135] Scheuerman, 2026.   [136] Scheuerman (2021, p. 10).   [137] Malm, 2021.

sabotage also increased the cost of an environmentally hazardous project. In general, SLT seeks to make these costs unbearable, so that corporate players will forgo environmentally damaging investments in the first place.

Crucially, SLT has successfully presented their sabotage actions as forms of "disarmament" to render weapons of ecological destruction inoperative, and as forms of land and water protection. This justification inscribes sabotage within a logic of defensive action, where it is the commons itself that is under threat. The Service Central du Renseignement Territorial, a French police-intelligence agency, has noted SLT's "perfectly mastered communication strategies," which persuade activists committed to nonviolence to instead adopt "civil resistance" – another term for what I am calling uncivil disobedience.[138]

Lai and Lim articulate the philosophical argument behind this turn to direct action or uncivil disobedience, arguing that civil disobedience (for instance, blocking highways or, as XR did in London in 2019, occupying the tube) indiscriminately and negatively affects people – most of whom are "innocent" when it comes to causing global warming and unable to effect policy change.[139] In contrast, uncivil disobedience such as sabotage of pipelines or of ecologically destructive construction projects can selectively target culpable agents themselves – extracting and polluting industries. For this reason, acts of uncivil disobedience on behalf of environmental protection satisfy better than their civil counterparts the fairness-based demand that responsible agents – not the broad public but captains of industry – be the ones to bear the burdens of tackling injustice.

7.2.3 Self-Violence

Neither accounts of civil disobedience nor the framework of defensive action seems to fit self-destructive resistance (as I dub tactics of resistance involving self-violence, including self-starvation, self-neglect, and self-immolation), a repertoire to which philosophers have given too little attention. Self-destructive resistance differs from civil disobedience (as commonly conceived) in being directly injurious to persons – specifically, oneself; not necessarily illegal; and often perceived as extreme, irrational, and pathological, especially when fatal, thus potentially hindering the act's legibility as an address. And if the agent is the one voluntarily injuring herself, we can adduce that the harm is not defensive and that the framework of defensive action does not apply.

But this is too hasty. Consider first that agents engaged in self-destructive resistance often seek to shift to their target responsibility for the harms they inflict on themselves. Thus, the IRA and the Irish Catholic Church considered

---

[138] Décugis, 2022.   [139] Lai and Lim, 2023.

the deaths of Bobby Sands and the other hunger strikers to be "murders"
committed by British Prime Minister Margaret Thatcher (and thus deserving
of proper funeral rites, which aren't available to suicides). Those who self-
immolate in public also lay blame on the entity – usually the state government –
they deem culpable for inflicting pain and suffering on themselves and others.
For instance, Aaron Bushnell immolated himself outside the Israeli embassy in
Washington, DC, in March 2024, to protest the killing of Palestinians in Gaza by
Israel, acts supported by the US government through its military, financial, and
diplomatic aid. Given that self-destructive resistance targets entities the resistor
deems culpable, the permissibility of their action would seem at least in part to
be a function of whether the entity in question really is culpable. The framework
of self-defense may thus be applied to assess the target's liability.

The harms inflicted in the course of self-destructive resistance may be
multiple. These include not only the harms inflicted by and on the agent herself,
but also the coercive pressure and burdens imposed on the target, as well as the
emotional pain and trauma experienced by loved ones and direct witnesses. The
harms of self-destructive resistance may be better described as "protective" and
"expressive," rather than "defensive." They are initiated by the self-destructive
resister to protect her and/or other victims' basic interests, including by expressing her/their freedom and dignity and defiance of the state.

Are these self-harms necessary to protect agents' and victims' interests?
Agents engaged in self-destructive resistance often lay claim to necessity by
presenting their act as a last resort. Abdellatif Laâbi, the Moroccan poet and
dissident who spent decades behind bars, defended his and fellow dissidents'
hunger strikes in these terms:

> the only weapon we've left
> is this irrepressible
> breath still inside us
> which we push to the furthest of limits
> risking its death
> to safeguard our dignity[140]

Especially in carceral contexts, the notion that there is little or no alternative to
self-destructive protests resonates. Whether the self-destructive harm is further
reasonably expected to be effective depends on a host of factors about the
specific tactic of self-destructive resistance elected, the context, and the goal
sought. But evidence shows that hunger strikes in prison are effective at
bringing about redress and reforms, for instance.[141] What is more, if the goal

---

[140] Laâbi, 2016.   [141] Delmas, 2024.

is to protect the dignity of the agent undertaking self-destructive resistance, then the expressive act's success conditions can easily be met.

Finally, it is reasonable to apply a proportionality test to cases of self-destructive resistance. One question is whether the threat of and actual harms of oppression are greater than the self-inflicted harm; another is whether the target is liable to the burdens imposed by agents engaged in self-destructive resistance. Incarcerated agents engaged in self-destructive resistance burden authorities by failing to follow the mandatory schedule of activities and disrupting prison order (hence the designation of self-destructive protests as disciplinary infractions). They also exert coercion by threatening their own life should their demands not be granted and are thus often condemned as "blackmail."

Steve McQueen's film *Hunger* (2004) begins with a dramatic and graphic rendition of the Dirty Protest at Long Kesh. The film shows filthy, resolute prisoners wearing nothing but a blanket, smearing their excrements on the walls of their cells and pouring urine under their cell door, and guards forced to work in the abject world created by the prisoners, washing the hallways in hazmat suits. The harms protesters inflicted on themselves and the burdens they imposed on prison officers could be deemed proportionate and justified in comparison with the course of inaction, since the protesters sought to preserve and affirm the dignity that the new policy threatened. In contrast, Norwegian mass murderer Anders Breivik's hunger strike to demand that authorities upgrade his video game system and let him play "more adult games" illustrates a disproportionate and unjustified act of self-destructive resistance.

It is thus possible and illuminating to apply the framework of defensive action – especially Pasternak's version – to cases of self-destructive resistance. Such application, however, calls for further refinements to the theoretical framework to account for, inter alia, the special circumstances under which agents may be motivated to draw from the repertoire of self-destructive resistance.

• • •

This section has challenged the conceptual binary violence/nonviolence to make room for the distinct categories of property damage and self-violence. On the standard account of civil disobedience, an act of principled lawbreaking that involves defensive force, damage to property, or self-violence cannot qualify as civil. In my view, it qualifies instead as uncivil disobedience. But since there is no overarching justificatory account of uncivil disobedience, such labeling does not help settle the essential question of normative permissibility. The section has put forth analytical tools to help with the latter task. The next section pivots toward the relation that principled disobedients entertain and should entertain toward law enforcement.

8 Sanctions against Disobedients

How should the state treat principled disobedients? Are principled disobedients morally bound to accept legal sanctions? This section begins with some canonical answers to the first question, reviewing both the jurisprudence that views civil disobedience as a public wrong worthy of punishment and the philosophical accounts that propose to tolerate and even carve a constitutional space for civil disobedience. I then clarify the demands that civility imposes on principled disobedients faced with the state's enforcement and administration of the law – motivating here the conceptual shift I have assumed thus far from the requirement to "accept punishment" to that of "non-evasion" – and defend deliberate, uncivil evasions from law enforcement and punishment.[142]

8.1 Civil Disobedience as Public Wrong

Many argue that civil disobedience should be understood as a wrongful act from the standpoint of law. Unlike its cousin, conscientious objection, civil disobedience has no legal existence; it is, in and of itself, unrecognized by law – a "legally unidentified object," in the jurist Clémence Demay's phrase.[143] Civil disobedience involves lawbreaking, and so civil disobedients are subject to criminal punishment, but not for civil disobedience itself.

At the same time, a jurisprudence has arisen around acts of civil disobedience – a jurisprudence concerned with whether the intent to disobey law, for principled reasons, could be a reason to treat a defendant leniently or else to sanction her that much more harshly. In particular, the destabilizing potential of civil disobedience and its perceived impermissibility in democracies that afford citizens lawful avenues of dissent pervade this jurisprudence. For example, judges in the nineteenth-century United States who harshly sanctioned Abolitionists breaking the law to aid slaves sometimes did so on the grounds that their actions would inflame the Southern states, leading to instability and even secession.[144] Decades later, civil rights activists protesting the racial caste system were presented as seditious "rabble-rousers" endangering political stability and undermining the rule of law with their disobedient activities.[145]

---

[142] This section draws from Delmas (2019 and 2025), where I focus on criminal law and constitutional law, respectively.

[143] Demay, 2022.   [144] Lippman, 1994.   [145] Sarat, 2014.

With respect to impermissibility, officials and judges have argued that the lawbreaking attending civil disobedience must be punished harshly because to do otherwise would imperil the democratic process by undermining its exclusive role in legal reform. A US appellate court faced with antiwar defendants convicted of violating the Military Selective Service Act of 1967 by "seizing Selective Service registration cards with intent to destroy them" brought together the stability and democracy concerns thusly:

> We counsel ... that the fabric of our democratic society is fragile, that there are broad opportunities for peaceful and legal dissent, and that the power of the ballot, if used, is great. Peaceful and constant progress under the Constitution remains, in our view, the best hope for a just society.[146]

At least in the United States, legal theorists who want to concede the value and justification of civil disobedience, while still defending its punishment, make a proceduralist argument based on courts' proper functions. They note that, per the doctrine and law of the separation of powers, the legislative assembly alone is tasked with making and changing laws, whereas courts are concerned with enforcing the letter of the law, impartially and without considering the moral merits or demerits of that law. Andrew Sabl has advanced a related argument, from a realist perspective, advocating punishing agents' actions without examining their states of mind, to avoid incentivizing defendants to profess deep conscientious beliefs in the hope of acquittal or leniency.[147]

8.2 Judicial Leniency and Rights to Civil disobedience

If many theorists – including judges weighing in on the philosophy of law and governance – view civil disobedience as a public wrong, others insist that civil disobedience is a public good that should be tolerated or at least prosecuted leniently. Ronald Dworkin urges judges to engage in an open dialogue with civil disobedients and dismiss their charges after hearing their motivations, or to use their discretion in sentencing to impose minimal punishments.[148] Although Dworkin is keen to give civil disobedients a space to articulate substantial constitutional arguments, his proposal still amounts to letting judges evaluate the worthiness of individual civil disobedients' causes, which does not on its own guarantee judicial leniency (though such leniency may well materialize, and regularly does in lower courts). Arendt proposed a reform that would treat civil disobedients as lobbyists rather than lawbreakers – specifically, that they be heard before legislatures as opposed to courts.[149]

---

[146] United States v. Kroncke, 459 F.2d 697 (8th Cir. 1972).   [147] Sabl (2021, pp. 159–160).
[148] Dworkin, 1985.   [149] Arendt, 1972.

Some liberal and democratic theorists have argued that civil disobedients should never be presumed worthy of punishment. They defend a moral right to civil disobedience that is independent of any justifications attributed to a given exercise of the right. This moral right designates a protected sphere in which to engage in civil disobedience, justifiably or not, and entails a presumptive claim against censure and punishment. Just as the right of free speech protects illiberal and offensive speech, not just "good" speech, so a right to civil disobedience would protect civil disobedients who pursue illiberal, undemocratic, or otherwise problematic causes.

David Lefkowitz and William Smith support this view, basing the right to civil disobedience on the broader right to democratic political participation. Kimberley Brownlee also argues for a right to civil disobedience, but grounds it in the "principle of humanism," which holds that "society has a duty to honor the fact that we are reasoning and feeling beings capable of forming deep moral commitments" by allowing conscientious persons who find themselves burdened by law's demands to freely disobey these on the basis of their convictions.[150] For Brownlee, the right to civil disobedience entails a presumptive protection against all forms of state interference, not just punishment but also smaller forms of penalization such as fines. None of these defenses of a right to civil disobedience extends to a defense of a right to uncivil disobedience, given the more serious transgressions and harms that the latter can generate.

Smith has further articulated a policing philosophy that orients law enforcement strategies toward accommodation, rather than prevention or management, of civil disobedience. On his view, "the police should, where possible, cooperate with civilly disobedient activists in order to assist in their commission of a protest that is effective as an expression of their grievance against law or policy."[151] This means that activists and police should engage in a dialogue about how the civil disobedient action will unfold, from beginning to end, including, say, pre-negotiated arrests. Noting that the police is especially unlikely to adopt such accommodating approach in the face of anti-police protests like Black Lives Matter, Jake Monaghan argues that police responses to disobedient demonstrations should be guided by a principle of proportionality, which requires de-escalating tactics – a principle that common crowd control police tactics like cordons and skirmish lines blatantly violate.[152]

---

[150] Lefkowitz, 2007; Brownlee (2012, p. 7); Smith (2013, chap. 4).   [151] Smith (2013, p. 111).
[152] Monaghan, 2023.

With this background in place, let's turn to our next question: how should principled disobedients relate to law enforcement, including efforts to arrest and prosecute them?

8.3 (Non-)Evasion in the Street, Jail, and Courtroom

Recall Socrates's refusal of Crito's offer to escape, despite the injustice of Socrates's death sentence. Like the requirement of publicity, the demand of non-evasion is motivated in large part by the imperative that disobedients demonstrate to the public the sincerity of their conviction as well as their respect for the rule of law, if not for the particular laws they have broken.[153]

Most philosophers endorse the requirement to accept punishment without elaborating on what it entails exactly. Those theorists who have discussed the requirement have tended to focus on questions related to the criminal trial: Must civil disobedients welcome their sentence without complaint or can they protest unfair punishment?[154] Is an appeal to legal defenses compatible with civil disobedience's requirement to accept punishment?[155] Must civil disobedients plead "guilty" or "not guilty"?[156] As these questions indicate, theorists have proceeded as though civil disobedients typically went to trial, and they have reduced the demands of civility to the willing acceptance of legal sanctions, presumed to be the verdict and sentence dispensed at trial.[157]

Yet most principled disobedients, like their "criminal" counterparts, never go to trial. Participants in public demonstrations, who are usually charged with Class A violations such as disorderly conduct and trespass, often have their charges dropped; or their case is dismissed; or they are issued an Adjournment in Contemplation of Dismissal (ACD) or Release on One's Recognizance (ROR), which simply requires defendants to remain offense-free for a set period (typically six months to a year) to have their case dismissed and the record sealed.[158] This would suggest that only disobedient defendants charged with serious offenses (even unjustly so) and tried are really in a position to satisfy the demand of civility – an odd and counterintuitive implication.

Whereas the requirement to willingly accept the punishment focuses on the judicial phase (with the question of pleas, defenses, and reactions to the verdict), the concept of "non-evasion" is better suited to capture the series of expectations corresponding to different stages of the face-off with the state. Non-evasion demands that the civil disobedient, during the action, (1) risk arrest by disobeying

---

[153] Cohen, 1966.   [154] Fortas, 1968; Cohen, 1971; Woozley, 1976.

[155] Bauer & Eckerstrom, 1987; McEwen, 1990; Sabl, 2001; Horder, 2004; Brownlee, 2012.

[156] Hall, 2007; Moraro, 2012 and 2018.

[157] I develop the argument sketched in this Section in Delmas forthcoming.

[158] Thomas-Hébert, 2020.

the law publicly and (2) either voluntarily submit to or else passively resist arrest; in jail, (3) cooperate with the detention and booking procedures; in court, (4) willingly appear before the judge when summoned, and (5) respect rules of courtroom decorum. It is plausible to hold that liberal civility implies all five demands, yet only the first one has been theorized, in the context of the publicity requirement.

Indeed, the demands that theorists have focused on – the question of pleas, criminal defenses, and reactions to the verdict – are not specified by civility: civil disobedients may have good principled or prudential reasons to plead "guilty" or "not guilty," they may appeal to criminal defenses, and they may complain about a harsh sentence without reneging their civil disobedient status. Meanwhile, critics of the duty to accept punishment tend to conflate the question of the permissibility of evading arrest and sanctions with the conceptual question, what makes an act of disobedience civil?[159] In what follows I both clarify each demand of non-evasion and defend the permissibility, under some circumstances, of evasion in the street, jail, and courtroom.

First, non-evasion demands risking arrest by publicly disobeying the law. Risking arrest applies to civil as well as uncivil disobedience. But by disobeying publicly, the agent puts her body on the line in a different way than covert disobedients might: she is visible and vulnerable to law enforcement and publicly demonstrates her willingness to risk sanctions. There may be reasons not to disobey publicly, but to do so anonymously and covertly, but this public and open stance in the street marks the civility of the disobedient agent.

The second component of non-evasion regards arrest, which is the last tool in the arsenal of law enforcement to control protests. Arrests usually come after various police orders have been issued, such as orders to stay on the sidewalk, get in the pen, show identification, or cease and disperse. Civil disobedients do not need to comply with police orders – indeed, there would be no lawbreaking if protesters abided police orders in the case of public demonstrations.

However, civility demands submitting to arrest. Fleeing or hiding to avoid arrest, helping others avoid arrest, and forcefully resisting arrest amount to evasive, uncivil conduct and are incompatible with civil disobedience. Passive resistance to arrest is different: it should be recognized as basically non-evasive and compatible with civil disobedience. Tactics commonly associated with civil disobedience and taught in nonviolence training workshops such as "going limp" or chaining oneself to equipment are classified in penal law as "Resisting Arrest" or "Obstructing Governmental Administration in the Second Degree" because they slow down police and make their work more difficult. Yet

---

[159] Brownlee, 2012; Moraro, 2012; Scheuerman, 2015; 2018.

they effectively enable the disobedient to continue their dissent past the action itself, by focusing attention on the state's forceful response to peaceful protests.

While civility demands non-evasion of law enforcement, much covert principled disobedience, such as clandestine provision of abortion services where it is illegal, requires evading law enforcement, by operating underground and maintaining strict security protocols to evade encounters with police and the criminal justice system. Evasion, in many cases like this, is a condition for the possibility of achieving the disobedient agent's goal. It is also a potentially permissible decision when the disobedient knows they will face very harsh and disproportionate criminal charges. Under the Animal Enterprise Terrorism Act (AETA), for instance, animal welfare activists have faced "terrorism" charges, even for acts that did not cause physical harm to people. In one infamous case, seven activists associated with the Stop Huntingdon Animal Cruelty (SHAC), a campaign to close one animal-testing firm, were convicted and sentenced in 2006 to four to six years in federal prison, solely for their online advocacy (coverage and support of protests that others carried out).[160]

Once arrested, protesters are brought to jail where they are detained and processed through the booking procedures. They will be held in a cell, identified, photographed, fingerprinted, strip searched, and interrogated. Civility arguably demands cooperating with police in jail by accepting detention and willingly sharing one's identity, so as to demonstrate that one stands by and is willing to answer to one's public disobedience. Noncompliance is likely to lead to forceful police response and put the arrestee in danger. However, civility does not require truthfully answering all the police questions at interrogation, and some forms of refusals to cooperate are compatible with civil disobedience and potentially justifiable as protests against mistreatment by the police.

The requirement to willingly appear before the judge when summoned for arraignment appears essential for civil disobedients, who would otherwise appear like criminals on the run. A "failure to appear warrant" would be filed against them, their driver's license could be immediately suspended, the police would look for them, and they would be held without bail upon their re-arrest. Again, a disobedient may have good reasons to evade criminal justice proceedings – the injustice of the charges, the expectation that they would not get a fair trial, and the likelihood of severe sanctions being some of them – but they could not be considered a civil disobedient if they did.

Finally, the requirement to respect rules of courtroom decorum translates civility into the courtroom, demanding the disobedient defendant demonstrate her overall respect for legality by abiding the rules of courtroom decorum –

---

[160] Hall, 2009.

rules that instruct defendants to stand up or sit, address the judge with her proper honorific, remain silent unless explicitly allowed to speak, solely answer the questions asked at the witness stand, and so on. This demand of civility entails that the paradigmatic uncivil conduct is "contempt of court," which includes heckling, interrupting, and refusing to obey judges' orders. Principled disobedients have often been punished specifically for such violations. For instance, in 1969, Black Panther Party chairman Bobby Seale repeatedly interrupted the proceedings of what came to be known as the Chicago Eight Conspiracy Trial to demand legal representation, which he hadn't been granted. He was gagged and shackled during the trial, charged with sixteen counts of contempt, and sentenced to four years in prison.[161]

This facet of non-evasion is, as Medina taught us, contextual and gradual. Courtroom rules vary from one setting (state and jurisdiction) to the next, and whether and how they are followed and enforced might greatly vary, depending on the judicial culture and the judge. Courtroom decorum is also a matter of degree: appearing to court in the "wrong" attire (say, wearing a t-shirt with a political slogan) is a minor violation, and it may well be ignored. It will typically take an accumulation of violations of courtroom decorum to describe a disobedient agent as "uncivil" in the courtroom. And as Seale's example makes clear, the judge may wield his discretionary power to keep order in the courtroom unfairly and unreasonably. The case also shows the flipside of the demands of civility in the courtroom, namely, the possibility for disobedient agents to weaponize the latter space for political purposes. If non-evasion in the form of courtroom decorum manifests respect for law, then incivility such as contempt of court may be justified to express disrespect toward the legal system, when the latter doesn't deserve our respect. Black Power defendants like Seale thus viewed the courtroom as a "hegemonic white space" and site of resistance.[162]

• • •

This section addressed the central twin issues of the state's proper, rights-respecting treatment of principled disobedients and of disobedient agents' expected response to the state's enforcement and administration of the law. The discussion revealed that principled disobedience does not emerge out of a vacuum, polished and frictionless, but takes shape through the course of events that also involve the legislature, police, district attorneys, and judges.

Beyond theorists' endorsement or critique of the requirement to accept punishment, which narrowly focuses on the trial, I proposed to conceptualize

---

[161] Bell, 2022.　　[162] Bell, 2022.

non-evasion to capture the demands of civility corresponding to different stages of the face-off with the state, in the street, jail, and courtroom. Ultimately, a stringent application of the non-evasion requirements threatens to undermine the goals of disobedience. Disobedients aim, after all, to defy the state. Escaping arrest and sanctions, rejecting judicial proceedings, and engaging in contempt of court can serve to promote a movement and express disobedient agents' distrust toward the state. Theorists might do well to focus their attention on the courtroom as a space of dissident praxis. They would find here a range of actions no less principled than those that placed the disobedient's case on the docket in the first place.

9 Defending Uncivil Disobedience

Uncivil disobedience, like civil disobedience, challenges the state's use of power, the political decisions made by legislators, and the democratic deficits of allegedly self-governing states. But in eschewing civility, protesters amplify the destabilizing potential of their disobedience. They also risk alienating potential allies and undermining the civic bonds among citizens. For these reasons, many scholars argue that, even if uncivil disobedience is sometimes permissible, it is generally unproductive and can never be superior to civil disobedience. Here, I examine and respond to these objections and argue for the distinct uses of incivility in resistance.

9.1 Is Uncivil Disobedience Counterproductive?

William Scheuerman, whose critique of the concept of uncivil disobedience as an "amorphous categorical rubric" we examined in Section 3, also chastises defenders of uncivil disobedience for ignoring its "ambivalent, oftentimes unsettling historical record."[163] In his view, theorists who defend uncivil disobedience neglect the social scientific evidence demonstrating the superior efficacy of civil disobedience and nonviolent protest across all sociopolitical contexts and the counterproductivity of uncivil, confrontational, and violent tactics. A social movement that relies on uncivil tactics is doomed to fail at the essential task of moral suasion: instead of winning the hearts of potential allies, an uncivil movement will alienate them, and thus undermine its chances of success.

Erica Chenoweth and Maria Stephan's research provides empirical ballast for this widely accepted idea. Analyzing 323 civil resistance campaigns between 1900 and 2006, 106 of them nonviolent and the rest violent, they found that

---

[163] Scheuerman (2019, p. 992).

nonviolent campaigns succeeded 65 percent of the time, while violent campaigns succeeded about 35 percent of the time.[164] What might explain this apparent divergence in fortunes? For one thing, a social movement benefits from as much popular participation as possible, and nonviolence lowers the bar for mass participation. In contrast, violent disobedience – and incivility more broadly – tends to depress movement turnout, by forcing participants to risk injury and arrest. In addition, those who oppose violence and incivility in principle will choose not to participate. Then too, uncivil and violent campaigns tend to galvanize security forces and the movement's opponents – the regime and its supporters – instead of giving security forces reasons to defect and side with the movement. Finally, while nonviolent campaigns are sometimes violently repressed, violent campaigns are very likely to be met with such repression, which the public is likely to see as justified.

Yet, without dismissing the power of nonviolence, the social scientific wisdom about violent and uncivil disobedience is subject to challenges. As Chenoweth and Stephan themselves acknowledge, their sample is subject to selection bias: nonviolent campaigns crushed in their infancy are not included in the dataset, because they seldom receive media coverage, whereas violent campaigns that are quashed early are more likely to be reported upon. What is more, the authors classify as nonviolent various resistance movements that do, in fact, harbor violent elements, such as the Philippines democracy movement of 1983–1986, the anti-Apartheid movement, the Second Intifada, and the Arab Spring. It is not necessarily unreasonable to consider a mostly nonviolent campaign nonviolent on the whole. But this shouldn't obscure the role that low-level violence, and the violent flanks of otherwise-nonviolent movements, might play in reaching successful outcomes. For instance, historians of the Black freedom struggle increasingly recognize the productivity of uncivil and threatening elements alongside and within the Civil Rights Movement.

Chenoweth and Stephan's dataset also is limited to "maximalist" civil resistance campaigns, defined as major resistance movements seeking to topple a dictator, oust an occupier, or achieve territorial independence. Resistance campaigns that demand legal reforms or cultural change (such as SlutWalks and #MeToo); protests against economic inequality and austerity; and movements for land reform, prison abolition, climate activism, and so on are not maximalist in this sense, though they may well be radical and even revolutionary in their outlook. As a result, the data tell us nothing about these campaigns, yet Chenoweth and Stephan have applied their findings to contemporary non-maximalist resistance movements, condemning any kind of violence in protest.

---

[164] Chenoweth and Stephan, 2011.

Conceiving of self-defense as "counterviolence," they urge protesters not to protect themselves or each other.[165] Such warnings should give us pause, especially as their effect is to legitimate the branding of peaceful protests as violent whenever protesters defend themselves from violence. As Avia Pasternak further notes, the data about the efficacy of nonviolence is, in fact, much "less conclusive when the resisting group is an oppressed minority," such as undocumented migrants or incarcerated persons, "rather than a group that enjoys fairly broad popular support," which shows again the limits of Chenoweth and Stephan's argument.[166]

As well, whether a civil resistance campaign succeeds may be hard to discern. If all we are concerned about is regime change, then it is relatively easy to say whether a movement succeeds or fails (though that too can be a controversial matter). But non-maximalist protests may seek to do many things at once, any of which can be more or less successful. The campaign may hope to draw the government's and the public's attention to an issue, build or galvanize a movement, bring about reforms, revise principles of political morality, and so on. Meanwhile, many types of uncivil disobedience are not primarily communicative: assisting migrants seeking to cross borders, providing abortions where they are criminalized, and rescuing animals from abuse, for example. The success of these actions can't be measured in terms of legal reforms, let along regime change.

Finally, Chenoweth has recently observed a concerning downward trend since 2006 in the success rates of "people-power movements," as they now call civil resistance movements. Drawing on the continually updated Nonviolent and Violent Campaign Outcomes (NAVCO) data, they found that "although mass mobilization has indeed persisted and even increased in quantity" between 2006 and 2020, "the success rates of nonviolent resistance have plummeted."[167] As they argue, the global COVID-19 pandemic has exacerbated and thrown in stark relief an array of authoritarian strategies deployed against people-power movements since the turn of the twenty-first century. These authoritarian strategies include restrictions on public gatherings and limits on peaceful assembly and free speech; emergency declarations suspending civil liberties and expanding executive powers; and the diffusion of "smart repression" techniques including digital repression, divide-and-conquer strategies playing on and exacerbating polarized politics, propaganda and misinformation. All governments, not only recognizably autocratic ones, have

---

[165] Chenoweth and Stephan, 2019.   [166] Pasternak (2025, p. 89).
[167] Chenoweth (2022, p. 305).

used this toolkit, though to varying degrees, to surveil and deter dissidents and to demobilize and suppress protest movements.

If available social science research does not conclusively show that uncivil disobedience is counterproductive, there is also some reason to believe uncivil disobedience can be even more productive than civil disobedience. Pasternak notes that while there is no evidence that the use of violent tactics increases domestic social movements' long-term effectiveness, there is evidence that violence can help movements achieve short-term gains, such as attracting substantial media attention and boosting morale among movement participants.[168] A movement may also benefit from a diversity of tactics, with each deployed when contextually useful. In addition, the presence of radical and violent elements tends to pressure authorities to negotiate with the mainstream of the movement. All of this can contribute to the work of bringing about lasting change.

9.2 A Unique Role for Uncivil Disobedience

The second central objection to the use of uncivil tactics in basically liberal democracies treats incivility as incompatible with the duties of civic friendship – the relations of mutual respect and forbearance among citizens living in societies marked by pluralism and difference.[169] For Rawls, "the duty of civility imposes a due acceptance of the defects of institutions and a certain restraint in taking advantage of them."[170] This restraint serves to maintain ties of "mutual trust and confidence" among citizens, fostering a bond based on "one's sincerity, for it is not easy to convince another that one's acts are conscientious, or even to be sure of this before oneself."[171]

In response to this objection, one might point out that some forms of uncivil disobedience, such as government whistleblowing, are unlikely to undermine civic friendship (though it might well diminish trust in institutions). But let us grant that uncivil tactics can indeed undermine civic friendship. An interesting question that follows is whether undermining civic friendship could be justified. I submit that it can be – that there is a place for threats to civic friendship in liberal democratic societies when the following conditions apply: the public is assured of the state's commitment to respecting everyone's full and equal status, a commitment typically embedded in a constitution or other basic law that guides institutional design and lawmaking; some citizens are effectively (de facto, if not de jure) denied full and equal status; and the injustice of this denial is not publicly recognized, perhaps because that injustice is not deliberate but results from the

---

[168] Pasternak (2025, pp. 96–105).   [169] This sub-section draws from Delmas (2020a).
[170] Rawls (1999, p. 312).   [171] Rawls (1999, p. 322).

interplay of social practices and institutional structures, as in cases of structural injustice, or because it simply doesn't seem like an injustice at all (think of felon disenfranchisement or enforcement of immigration law).

Under these circumstances, the majority may be and feel bound by civic friendship, but from the perspective of oppressed minorities, civic friendship is an illusion. The oppressed minority might then fruitfully resort to civil disobedience, although it very well may be perceived as uncivil. One way or another, uncivil disobedience may be better suited than civil disobedience to the goal of radically disrupting the status quo and gripping the public's attention. Where civil disobedients typically seek to coax and persuade, uncivil disobedients can jolt – they can compel the community to confront the disconnect between reality and professed ideals. A peaceful march for civil rights or a Black Lives Matter die-in – instances of civil disobedience – can do this. But an uprising, including targeted property destruction and expressions of anger directed at the police, conveys the community's rage at society's lack of concern for Black poverty and Black death in more jarring ways. Uncivil protests, in certain contexts, do not so much threaten and undermine civic friendship as expose its absence.

By protesting uncivilly, agents question the rules of public engagement and their exclusionary effects. They contest and disrupt the moral and political consensus. This kind of uncivil disruption may set back activists' cause by reducing popular support. But even where it is futile or counterproductive, uncivil disobedience may still have intrinsic value as a fitting expression of warranted frustration and distrust. These attitudes are especially worth communicating to fellow oppressed people, who may take confidence from expressions of solidarity. And the expressions of disrespect and anger toward legal and political authority that are characteristic of uncivil disobedience may be seen as assertions of agency and dignity in the face of threats to both.

•••

The idea that uncivil disobedience undermines the civic bonds among citizens and is counterproductive buttresses the widespread calls for civility in protest not only by condemning uncivil tactics but also by *predicting* their failure. This reasoning facilitates the unfolding of a self-fulfilling prophecy of sorts, as observers and potential allies might be cautious to join or support a movement that they have been assured will fail. This widespread view of uncivil disobedience's counterproductivity supports the status quo that activists are trying to unsettle by restricting the repertoire of acceptable tactics they may use in the process. It thus adds to the activists' task of trying to effect social change an extra – and unfair – burden of working with or around the common rejection of incivility. Amia Srinivasan has argued that the common notion that anger is counterproductive works to stifle its value as a source of motivation, self-respect, and knowledge, and to erase its intrinsic aptness, in this way constituting a second-order, affective injustice added to the first-order structural socio-political injustice confronting victims of oppression.[172] We might similarly argue that the common view of incivility imposes unfair demands on activists, such as tone policing, that obscure the fact noted above that domestic movements by highly marginalized groups, even when they are exclusively nonviolent and civil, often fail. Justice requires revising the demands made on protesters.

Conclusion

In exploring the resonances and dissonances between theories and practices of civil disobedience, we see that much of what is understood as civil disobedience is not, in fact, civil in the common liberal sense of civility. Some of the historical exemplars of civil disobedience – from the Boston Tea Party to anarchist direct action – bear the marks of uncivil, more so than civil, disobedience. The widespread intuition that certain uncivil actions are nonetheless morally permissible speaks to the vital importance of a more encompassing philosophy of disobedience, one that can address uncivil, as well as civil, action. After all, the philosophy of disobedience is supposed to guide behavior and judgment – to provide tools for orienting practice and normatively evaluating it.

Fortunately, theorists of disobedience have lately paid more attention to incivility. They argue that uncivil disobedience can be justified even under liberal democratic conditions, and a fortiori in contexts of democracies that are backsliding into "competitive authoritarian" regimes.[173] They defend uncivil disobedience on the grounds that it can help to achieve morally defensible goals, such as redressing injustice, realizing rescue and mutual aid, and affirming agency and dignity. But what about when disobedience, civil or uncivil, serves other, regressive, exclusionary, and indefensible goals? Thus far, my analysis has not touched on such cases.

As a threshold matter, there exists doubt as to whether such disobedience could, in the first place, be civil. Albert Ogien asserts, "Civil disobedience *always* serves to increase people's social and political rights. We have *never* seen civil disobedience being used to suppress people's rights."[174] Ogien looks to the example of officials who have refused to issue marriage licenses to

---

Srinivasan, 2016.

the concept of competitive authoritarianism, see Levitsky and Way (2020).

wed in Perrot, 2017. My translation and emphasis.

same-sex couples where these couples have a right to marry. Making a radical democratic argument, he contends that these acts of refusal cannot constitute civil disobedience *insofar as* they seek to prevent rather than expand the exercise of rights. Manuel Cervera-Marzal, another radical democrat, draws a similarly sharp contrast between disobedience on the political left and right, situating civil disobedience solely on the left, and stressing its pursuit of equality. Right-wing disobedience, on this version of radical democracy, should be understood as conscientious objection. Cervera-Marzal thus insists that disobedience on the right is not political. It is instead the work of individuals acting in isolation, on the basis of their conscience, not to ask that the law be changed but that they be exempted from it.[175]

Such views strike me as narrowminded in the face of disagreements about justice. As theories, they are also unhelpful and misguided because they deny both that right-wing social movements exist and that they have used civilly disobedient tactics. Yet abundant evidence indicates otherwise. Movements against reproductive rights and LGBTQ+ rights are clearly both large and active, and they have deployed civil and uncivil forms of disobedience (as well as terror tactics). Likewise, opponents (many on the right) of the public health measures that authorities took to slow down the spread of COVID-19 made frequent use of civil disobedient tactics, such as gathering publicly in violation of confinement orders. To view these protests as aggregates of conscientious objectors would be to engage in the same fallacy that Arendt denounced in the case of anti-Vietnam War activism, namely, "the assumption that we are dealing with individuals, who pit themselves subjectively and conscientiously against the laws and customs of the community," when "the fact is that we are dealing with organized minorities" formed "with the same spirit that has informed voluntary associations."[176]

While civil disobedience has historically been associated with social justice causes, its tactics can be directed toward many different ends. This reality militates in favor of the liberal account of civil disobedience, which distinguishes its definition from its justification. While democratic theorists define and defend all at once, conceiving of civil disobedience as democratic empowerment, liberals narrowly define civil disobedience as a communicative breach of law, constrained by the requirements of publicity, nonviolence, and non-evasion. This view provides solid grounds to defend everyone's right to engage in civil disobedience, even those with whom we vehemently disagree. Recognizing others' right to practice civil disobedience even in the service of causes to which one objects – but not uncivil disobedience, given the heavier

---

[175] Interviewed in Perrot, 2017. My translation.   [176] Arendt (1972, p. 104).

burdens and costs it might impose – seems essential in a pluralistic environment, where people hold competing conceptions of the common good and of justice, as well as conflicting interpretations of constitutional basics.

In this plural world, it is defenses of uncivil disobedience that raise a potentially significant concern, as such defenses may encourage citizens to take matters in their own hands in potentially unconstrained ways every time they think they are witnessing injustice. Citizens who self-appoint as legislators, in this context, risk becoming a dangerous horde of vigilantes. This concern materialized in the United States on January 6, 2021, for instance, when a mob comprising white nationalists, neo-Nazis, adherents of the QAnon conspiracy, and far-right militiamen from the ranks of the Proud Boys, Three Percenters, Boogaloo Bois, Last Sons of Liberty, and Oath Keepers stormed the Capitol in Washington, DC, to prevent the certification of the Electoral College vote in favor of president-elect Joe Biden.

The January 6 riot, inflamed by Donald Trump in the wake of his election loss and carried out by his supporters, represents a litmus test for justifications of uncivil disobedience, which it might certainly be seen as an instance of. Some, perhaps many, of the rioters were motivated by principles of political morality: they believed that the election had been "rigged" and "stolen" and, by ensuring that the rightful winner took office, sought to defend the US Constitution and the principles it embodies. They might argue that their attack on the Capitol aimed to redress injustice while restoring democratic legitimacy and the rule of law. Draped in American flags and symbols such as the Gadsden flag, with its coiled timber rattlesnake ready to strike, they saw themselves as patriotic descendants of the Boston Tea Party and the American Revolution.

Applying Pasternak's framework of defensive action, one might argue that the rioters thought, on the basis of the evidence available to them, that their attack on the Capitol was necessary and proportionate to protect President Trump from the denial of his legitimate claim to office. Indeed, Trump's supporters have consistently claimed to believe that he was so denied. For instance, a December 2023 poll found that two-thirds of Republicans thought Joe Biden was not legitimately elected, and 62 percent said there was solid evidence of widespread voter fraud in the 2020 election.[177] Could the storming of the Capitol building be justified, then? Were the harms inflicted during the riot defensive or "protective," in Pasternak's sense? The answer to both questions is negative.

---

[177] Washington Post-University of Maryland poll (December 14–18, 2023): www.washingtonpost
.com/documents/1f428bba-56ee-4800-b00d-7fd1b0004627.pdf?itid=lk_inline_manual_4.

For Pasternak, violence initiated by protesters during riots can be justified if they meet the necessity and proportionality tests as means to protect marginalized citizens' basic interests in safety, dignity, and political participation. But the rioters' basic interests were not thus threatened, and their aims were different. They came to the Capitol armed to the teeth, ready for war. They also sought retribution, as they threatened to hang Vice President Mike Pence for his willingness to certify electoral votes. The violence unleashed during the attack caused at least four deaths, hundreds of injuries, and about $1.5 million in property damage. The ensuing criminal charges against the rioters reflect the destruction they wrought: about one-third of the 1,200 or so defendants were charged with assault on or interference with law enforcement officers, and dozens were charged with theft or other property crimes, weapons offenses, and making threats. Along with several others, Oath Keepers founder Stewart Rhodes was convicted of seditious conspiracy; he was found by a judge to have committed an act of terrorism.

The magnitude of the violence unleashed as well as the attackers' aims – war and retribution, rather than defense – further cast doubt on the fittingness of the category of uncivil disobedience to approach this event. We might instead take seriously participants' own framing of the attack as an attempt to overthrow a tyrannical government, comporting with the right of revolution. Yet this right arises only when a government is tyrannical, a determination that is *not* in the eyes of the beholder: the right cannot be invoked on the basis of mistaken beliefs about a duly elected (though flawed) democratic government. There was demonstrably no evidence of widespread voter fraud enabling Biden's victory and no reason to believe that the process resulting in his election was unfair – or that it was more unfair than previous electoral processes, including the one that installed Trump in the Oval Office in the first place – and each of the rioters had ready access to this information. There was no right of revolution to vindicate on January 6.

The specter of January 6 need not cloud the philosophical defense of either civil or uncivil disobedience, for no reasonable defense of either could encompass what happened that day. But, of course, this does not mean we have carte blanche to disobey as and whenever we wish. Resistance by means of civil and uncivil disobedience demands a deep well of responsibility on the part of agents. In the current climate of creeping authoritarianism and governments' crackdown on dissent, it also demands much resoluteness and courage.

References

Allard-Tremblay, Y. (2026). Equivocal Resistance: Challenging the Colonial Apprehension of Indigenous Political Resistance. In *The Ethics of Uncivil Protest and Resistance*, C. Delmas and A. Pasternak (eds.). Oxford: Oxford University Press.

Applbaum, A. (2019). *Legitimacy: The Right to Rule in a Wanton World.* Cambridge: Harvard University Press.

Arendt, H. (1972). *Crises of the Republic: Lying in Politics, Civil Disobedience, On Violence, Thoughts on Politics and Revolution.* New York: Harcourt.

Bakunin, M. (1990 [1873]). *Statism and Anarchy,* M. S. Shatz and R. Geuss (eds.). Cambridge: Cambridge University Press.

Baldwin, J. (1966). A Report from Occupied Territory. *The Nation,* July 11.

Bauer, S. M. & Eckerstrom, P. J. (1987). The State Made Me Do It: The Applicability of the Necessity Defense to Civil Disobedience. *Stanford Law Review* 39: 1173–200.

Bedau, H. (ed.) (1991). *Civil Disobedience in Focus.* London: Routledge.

(1961). On Civil Disobedience. *The Journal of Philosophy* 58(21): 653–661.

Bell, J. (2022). Kangaroo Court: The Black Power Movement and the Courtroom as a Space of Resistance. *American Behavioral Scientist* 66(11): 1539–1557.

Bey, H. (2003 [1985]). *T.A.Z.: The Temporary Autonomous Zone, Ontological Anarchy, Poetic Terrorism.* Brooklyn: Autonomedia.

Bourdieu, P. (1977). *Outline of a Theory of Practice.* New York: Cambridge University Press.

Bové, J. and Luneau, G. (2004). *Pour la désobéissance civique.* Paris: Éditions La Découverte.

Brownlee, K. (2016). The Civil Disobedience of Edward Snowden: A Reply to William Scheuerman. *Philosophy and Social Criticism* 42(10): 965–970.

(2012). *Conscience and Conviction: The Case for Civil Disobedience.* Oxford: Oxford University Press.

Bulman-Pozen, J. and Pozen, D. (2015): Uncivil Obedience. *Columbia Law Review* 115: 809–872.

Celikates, R. (2021). Radical Democratic Disobedience. In *The Cambridge Companion to Civil Disobedience,* W. Scheuerman (ed.). New York: Cambridge University Press.

(2014). Civil Disobedience as a Practice of Civic Freedom. In *On Global Citizenship: James Tully in Dialogue*, D. Owen (ed.). London: Bloomsbury Press.

Chenoweth, E. (2022). Can Nonviolent Resistance Survive COVID-19? *Journal of Human Rights* 21(3): 304–316.

Chenoweth, E. and Stephan, M. (2019). Violence Is a Dangerous Route for Protesters. *Foreign Policy*, December 18.

(2011). *Why Civil Resistance Works: The Strategic Logic of Nonviolent Conflict*. New York: Columbia University Press.

Çıdam, Ç., Scheuerman, W. E., Delmas, C. et al. (2020). Theorizing the Politics of Protest: Contemporary Debates on Civil Disobedience. Contemporary Political Theory 19: 513–546.

Çıdam, Ç. (2021). *In the Street: Democratic Action, Theatricality, and Political Friendship*. New York: Oxford University Press.

Cobb, Charles E. 2014. *This Nonviolent Stuff'll Get You Killed: How Guns Made the Civil Rights Movement Possible*. New York: Basic Books.

Cohen, C. (1971). *Civil Disobedience: Conscience, Tactics, and the Law*. New York: Columbia University Press.

Davis, A. (1974). *Angela Davis: An Autobiography*. New York: International Publishers.

De Cleyre, V. (2004 [1912]). Direct Action. In *The Voltairine de Cleyre Reader*, A. J. Brigati (ed.). Oakland, CA: AK Press.

Décugis, J. M. (2022). Les Soulèvements de la Terre : révélations sur le fer de lance de l'écologie radicale en France. *Le Parisien*, December 20.

Delmas, C. and Brownlee, K. (2024). Civil Disobedience. In *The Stanford Encyclopedia of Philosophy*, E. N. Zalta & U. Nodelman (eds.).

Delmas, C. (2025). Civil Disobedience. In *The Cambridge Handbook of Constitutional Theory*, R. Bellamy and J. King (eds.). Cambridge University Press.

Delmas, C. (Forthcoming). From Acceptance of Punishment to (Non-)Evasion in Disobedience. Criminal Law and Philosophy.

(2024). The Right to Hunger Strike. *American Political Science Review* 118(2): 848–861.

(2020a). Uncivil Disobedience in Hong Kong. *Boston Review*, January 13.

(2020b). Uncivil Disobedience. In *NOMOS LXII: Protest and Dissent*, M. Schwartzberg (ed.). New York: New York University Press.

(2019). Civil Disobedience, Punishment, and Injustice. In *The Palgrave Handbook of Applied Ethics and the Criminal Law*, K. Kessler Ferzan and L. Alexander (eds.). Palgrave MacMillan.

(2018a). *A Duty to Resist: When Disobedience Should Be Uncivil*. New York: Oxford University Press.

(2018b). Is Hacktivism the New Civil Disobedience? *Raisons politiques* 69(1): 63–81.

Demay, C. (2022). *Le droit face à la désobéissance civile: Quelle catégorisation pour un « objet juridique non identifié »* ? Zürich, Schulthess.

Dworkin, R. (1985). *A Matter of Principle*. Cambridge, MA: Harvard University Press.

(1978). *Taking Rights Seriously*, 5th ed. Cambridge: Harvard University Press.

Edmundson, W. A. (1998). *Three Anarchical Fallacies*. Cambridge: Cambridge University Press.

Flanigan, E. T. (2023). Futile Resistance as Protest. *Mind* 132(527): 631–658.

Forrester, K. (2019). *In the Shadow of Justice: Postwar Liberalism and the Remaking of Political Philosophy*. Princeton: Princeton University Press.

Fortas, A. (1968). *Concerning Dissent and Civil Disobedience*. New York: Signet Broadside.

Foucault, M. (1983). The Subject and Power. In *Beyond Structuralism and Hermeneutics*, H. Dreyfus and P. Rabinow (eds.). Chicago: University of Chicago Press.

Franks, B. (2003) Direct Action Ethic. *Anarchist Studies* 11(1): 13–41.

Frowe, H. and Parry J. (2022). Self-Defense. In *The Stanford Encyclopedia of Philosophy*, E. N. Zalta (ed.).

Frowe, H. (2014). *Defensive Killing: An Essay on War and Self-Defence*. Oxford: Oxford University Press.

(2010). A Practical Account of Self- Defence. *Law and Philosophy* 29(3): 245–272.

Fung, A. (2005). Deliberation before the Revolution: Toward an Ethics of Deliberative Democracy in an Unjust World. *Political Theory* 33(2): 397–419.

Gandhi, M. (1973). *Selected Writings of Mahatma Gandhi*, R. Duncan (ed.). Glasgow: Fontana/Collins.

Graeber, D. (2009). *Direct Action. An Ethnography*. Oakland, CA: AK Press.

Gregg, R. B. (1960). *The Power of Nonviolence*, 2nd rev. ed. Canton, ME: Greenleaf Books.

Grimké, A. (2003). *Walking by Faith: The Diary of Angelina Grimké 1828-1835*. University of South Carolina Press.

(1838). *An Appeal to the Women of the Nominally Free State North*. Boston: Published by Isaac Knapp.

Gurley Flynn, E. (1917). *Sabotage: The Conscious Withdrawal of the Workers' Industrial Efficiency*. Chicago: IWW Publishing Bureau.

Habermas, J. (1985). Civil Disobedience: Litmus Test for the Democratic Constitutional State, Torpey, J. (trans.). *Berkeley Journal of Sociology* 30: 95–116.

Hall, M. R. (2007). Guilty but Civilly Disobedient: Reconciling Civil Disobedience and the Rule of Law. *Cardozo Law Review* 28: 2083–2132.

Hall, L. (2009). Disaggregating the Scare from the Greens. *Vermont Law Review* 33(4): 689–715.

Harcourt, B. (2012). The Politics of Incivility. *Arizona Law Review* 54(2): 345–373.

Hartman, S. (2019). *Wayward Lives, Beautiful Experiments: Intimate Histories of Riotous Black Girls, Troublesome Women, and Queer Radical.* New York: W. W. Norton

Havercroft, (2021). Why Is There No Just Riot Theory? *British Journal of Political Science* 51(3): 909–923.

Hooker, J. (2023). *Black Grief/White Grievance: The Politics of Loss.* Princeton: Princeton University Press.

Horder, J. (2004). *Excusing Crime*. Oxford: Oxford University Press.

Ingram, J. (2021). Anarchism: Provincializing Civil Disobedience. In *The Cambridge Companion to Civil Disobedience*, W. Scheuerman (ed.). New York: Cambridge University Press.

Jubb, R. (2019). Disaggregating Political Authority: What's Wrong with Rawlsian Civil Disobedience? *Political Studies* 67(4): 955–971.

Kessler Ferzan, K. (2018). Defending Honor and Beyond: Reconsidering the Relationship between Seemingly Futile Defense and Permissible Harming. *Journal of Moral Philosophy* 15(6): 683–705.

Kilgo, D. (2021). Media Bias Delegitimizes Black-Rights Protesters. *Nature* 593: 315.

King, M. L. K., Jr. (2010 [1968]). *Where Do We Go from Here? Chaos or Community.* Boston: Beacon Press.

(2000 [1964]). *Why We Can't Wait*. Signet Classics: Penguin Random House.

(1991 [1963]). Letter from Birmingham City Jail. In *Civil Disobedience in Focus*, H. Bedau (ed.). London: Routledge.

(1960). Suffering and Faith. *Christian Century* 77(27): 510.

Krug, Mercy J. A., Dahlberg L. L., and Zwi A. B. (2002). The World Report on Violence and Health. *The Lancet* 360 (9339): 1083–1088.

Laâbi, A. (2016). *Beyond the Barbed Wire: Selected Poems*, A. Naffis-Sahely (trans.). Manchester: Carcanet Press.

Lai, T.-H. (2020). Political Vandalism as Counter-Speech: A Defense of Defacing and Destroying Tainted Monuments. *European Journal of Philosophy* 28(3):602–616.

Lai, T.-H. and Lim, C.-M. (2023). Environmental Activism and the Fairness of Costs Argument for Uncivil Disobedience. *Journal of the American Philosophical Association* 9(3): 490–509.

Laugier, S. and Ogien, A. (2010). *Pourquoi désobéir en démocratie ?* Paris: La Découverte.

Lazar, S. (2012). Necessity in Self-Defense and War. *Philosophy & Public Affairs* 40(1): 3–44.

Lefkowitz, D. (2007). On a Moral Right to Civil Disobedience. *Ethics* 117(2): 202–233.

Lim, C.-M. (2020). Vandalizing Tainted Commemorations. *Philosophy and Public Affairs* 48(2): 185–216.

Lippman, M. (1994). Liberating the Law: The Jurisprudence of Civil Disobedience and Resistance. *San Diego Justice Journal* 2: 317-394.

McEwen, S. J., Jr. (1990). The Protester: A Sentencing Dilemma. *The Notre Dame Journal of Law, Ethics and Public Policy* 5: 987–993.

Monaghan, J. (2023). Policing Disobedient Demonstrations. *Criminal Law and Philosophy* 17: 653–668.

Morgan, E. S. (2012 [1956]). *The Birth of the Republic, 1763-1789*. Chicago: The University of Chicago Press.

Pasternak, A. (2025). *No Justice, No Peace: The Ethics of Violent Protests*. New York: Oxford University Press.

Perrot, A. (2017). La pensée désobéissante. *Désobéissance civile : citoyens hors la loi* (2/4). Podcast LSD La série documentaire. Paris: Radio France.

Levitsky, S. and Way, L. (2020). The New Competitive Authoritarianism. *Journal of Democracy* 31(1): 51-65.

Livingston, A. (2020). Power for the Powerless: Martin Luther King, Jr.'s Late Theory of Civil Disobedience. *The Journal of Politics* 82(2): 700–713.

Malm, A. (2021). *How To Blow Up a Pipeline*. London: Verso Books.

Mantena, K. (2018). Showdown for Nonviolence: The Theory and Practice of Nonviolence Politics. In *To Shape a New World: Essays on the Political Philosophy of Martin Luther King, Jr.*, T. Shelby and B. M. Terry (eds.). Cambridge, MA: Harvard University Press.

(2012). Another Realism: The Politics of Ghandian Nonviolence. *American Political Science Review* 106 (2): 255–470.

Marx, K. (1963). *The Poverty of Philosophy*. New York: International Publishers.

Medina, J. (2020). No Justice, No Peace: Uncivil Protest and the Politics of Confrontation. In *NOMOS LXII: Protest and Dissent*, M. Schwartzberg (ed.). New York: New York University Press.

Mills, C. W. (2007). White Ignorance. In S. Sullivan & N. Tuana (eds.), *Race and Epistemologies of Ignorance*. Albany: SUNY Press.

Moraro, P. (2018). On (Not) Accepting the Punishment for Civil Disobedience. *Philosophical Quarterly* 68(272): 503–520.

(2012). A Dilemma for the Civil Disobedient: Pleading "Guilty" or "Not Guilty" in the Courtroom? In *The Public in Law: Representations of the Political in Legal Discourse*, C. Michelon, C., Clunie, G., McCorkindale, C., and Psarras, H. (eds.). Edinburgh/Glasgow: Ashgate.

Nhat Hanh, T. (2022 [1967]). *Vietnam: Lotus in a Sea of Fire: A Buddhist Proposal for Peace*. Berkeley: Parallax Press.

Pineda, E. (2021a). *Seeing Like an Activist: Civil Disobedience and the Civil Rights Movement*. New York: Oxford University Press.

(2021b). Civil Disobedience, and What Else? Making Space for Uncivil Forms of Resistance. *European Journal of Political Theory* 20(1): 157–164.

Plato. (2002 [399 BCE]). *Crito*. In *Five Dialogs*, 2nd ed., J. M. Cooper (ed.), & G. M. A. Grube (trans.). Indianapolis: Hackett.

Pouget, E. (2003 [1903]). *Direct Action*. London: Kate Sharpley Library.

(1913). *Sabotage*, A. M. Giovannitti (trans.). Chicago, IL: Charles H. Kerr.

Rawls, J. (1999 [1971]). *A Theory of Justice*. Cambridge, MA: Harvard University Press. Revised Edition.

Renault, E. (2015). *The Experience of Injustice: A Theory of Recognition*. New York: Columbia University Press.

Sabl, A. (2021). Realist Disobedience. In *The Cambridge Companion to Civil Disobedience*, W. Scheuerman (ed.). New York: Cambridge University Press.

(2001). Looking Forward to Justice: Rawlsian Civil Disobedience and Its Non-Rawlsian Lessons. *Journal of Political Philosophy* 9(3): 307–330.

Sarat, A. (2014). Keeping Civility in Its Place: Dissent, Injustice, and the Lessons of History. In *Law, Society, and Community: Socio-Legal Essays in Honour of Roger Cotterrell*, R. Nobes and D. Schiff (eds.). London: Routledge.

Scalmer, S. (2023). Direct Action: The Invention of a Transnational Concept. *International Review of Social History* 68(3): 357–387.

Scheuerman, W. E. (2018). Civil Disobedience. Cambridge, UK, Medford, MA: Polity Press.

Scheuerman, W. E. (2026). *Property Disobedience as Protest: Rethinking Political Nonviolence*. Philadelphia: University of Pennsylvania Press.

(2021). Introduction: Why, Once Again, Civil Disobedience? In *The Cambridge Companion to Civil Disobedience*, W. Scheuerman (ed.). New York: Cambridge University Press.

(2019). Why Not Uncivil Disobedience? *Critical Review of International Social and Political Philosophy* 25(7), 980–999.

(2015). Recent Theories of Civil Disobedience: An Anti-Legal Turn? *Journal of Political Philosophy* 23(4): 427–449.

(2014). Whistleblowing as Civil Disobedience: The Case of Edward Snowden. *Philosophy and Social Criticism* 40(7): 609–628.

Sitrin, M. A. (2012). *Everyday Revolutions: Horizontalism and Autonomy in Argentina*. London: Zed Books.

Smith, W. (2021). Democratic Disobedience. In *The Cambridge Companion to Civil Disobedience*, W. Scheuerman (ed.). New York: Cambridge University Press.

(2013). *Deliberative Democracy and Civil Disobedience*. Abingdon: Routledge.

Souza dos Santos, E. (2024). *La désobéissance civile: Un essai de généalogie conceptuelle, 1866–1975*, Thèse soutenue à l'École Doctorale de Philosophie de l'Université Paris 1 Panthéon-Sorbonne.

Srinivasan, A. (2016). The Aptness of Anger. *The Journal of Political Philosophy* 26(2): 123–144.

Terry, B. M. (2018). MLK Now. *Boston Review*, September 10.

Thomas-Hébert, C. (2020). The Trump Resistance's Repertoire of Contention and its Conception and Practice of Civil Disobedience and Nonviolent Direct Action (2016–2018): An Institutionalization of Protest? *Society of Americanists Review* 2: 1–32.

Thoreau, H. D. (2001). *A Plea for Captain John Brown*. In *Essays: A Fully Annotated Edition*, ed. Jeffrey S. Cramer (New Haven, CT: Yale University Press, 2013) pp. 190–216.

(1991 [1866]). Civil Disobedience. In *Civil Disobedience in Focus*, H. Bedau (ed.). London: Routledge.

Umoja, A. O. (2013). *We Will Shoot Back: Armed Resistance in the Mississippi Freedom Movement*. New York: NYU Press.

Walzer, M. (1982). *Obligations: Essays on Disobedience, War, and Citizenship*. Cambridge, MA: Harvard University Press.

Williams, R. F. (1998 [1962]). *Negroes with Guns*. Detroit: Wayne State University Press.

Woodly, D. (2021). *Reckoning: Black Lives Matter and the Democratic Necessity of Social Movements*. Oxford: Oxford University Press.

Woozley, A. D. (1976). Civil Disobedience and Punishment. *Ethics* 86: 323–331.

Young, I. M. (2001). Activist Challenges to Deliberative Democracy. *Political Theory* 29(5): 670–690.

Zinn, H. (2011 [1997]). *The Zinn Reader: Writings on Disobedience and Democracy*. New York: Seven Stories Press.

Acknowledgment

I am deeply grateful to Avia Pasternak and Gina Schouten, whose friendship, conversations, and encouragement have been a constant source of inspiration.

To my colleague and friend Whitney Kelting — our seminar on anarchism was the highlight of my teaching career, and the central chapter bears its imprint.

To my husband Gabriel and our children, Marcel and Augustin, for their love and support. I promise I'm done writing on weekends!

To my students at Northeastern, to whom I dedicate this book.

For EU product safety concerns, contact us at Calle de José Abascal, 56–1°,
28003 Madrid, Spain or eugpsr@cambridge.org.